Leadership Skills for Project and Programme Managers

London: TSO

information & publishing solutions

Published by TSO (The Stationery Office) and available from:

Online
www.tsoshop.co.uk

Mail,Telephone, Fax & E-mail
TSO
PO Box 29, Norwich, NR3 1GN
Telephone orders/General enquiries: 0870 600 5522
Fax orders: 0870 600 5533
E-mail: customer.services@tso.co.uk
Textphone 0870 240 3701

TSO Shops
16 Arthur Street, Belfast BT1 4GD
028 9023 8451 Fax 028 9023 5401
71 Lothian Road, Edinburgh EH3 9AZ
0870 606 5566 Fax 0870 606 5588

TSO@Blackwell and other Accredited Agents

The information contained in this publication is believed to be correct at the time of manufacture. Whilst care has been taken to ensure that the information is accurate, the publisher can accept no responsibility for any errors or omissions or for changes to the details given.

Melanie Franklin and Susan Tuttle have asserted their moral rights under the Copyright, Designs and Patents Act 1988, to be identified as the authors of this work.

The Swirl logo™ is a Trade Mark of the Office of Government Commerce

PRINCE2™ is a Trade Mark of the Office of Government Commerce

The PRINCE2 Cityscape logo™ is a Trade Mark of the Office of Government Commerce in the United Kingdom and other countries

PRINCE® is a Registered Trade Mark of the Office of Government Commerce in the United Kingdom and other countries

MSP™ is a Trade Mark of the Office of Government Commerce

A CIP catalogue record for this book is available from the British Library

A Library of Congress CIP catalogue record has been applied for

First published 2008

ISBN 9780113310807

Printed in the United Kingdom by The Stationery Office, London

N5810791 c20 06/08

Contents

List of figures and tables

Acknowledgements

The ideas and content for this book are a result of our many years of experience in project and programme management. They are also a result of all the successes and failures we have had on our projects and programmes, and all of the stories and anecdotes we have collected over the years. However, we would specifically like to thank all of our colleagues, clients and associates whom we interviewed for this book (too numerous to mention), and Maurice Leppard and Lindsay Campbell for their many hours spent reading through the content.

REVIEWERS

Angela Berry	Information Services
Catherine East	Audit Commission
Neil Franklin	Department of Health
Ian Gotts	KPMG
Helen Goulding	Audit Commission
Angela Murphy	London Borough of Camden
Stefan Plocki	

MATURITY MARK

The TSO maturity mark on the back cover will help you decide if this publication is positioned at the appropriate level for your requirements and provide a route map to progress with embedding the OGC best-practice guidance. This publication, *Leadership Skills for Project and Programme Managers*, is levels 2 and 3.

Level 2 is Repeatable (process discipline) – OGC guidance is used repeatedly.

Level 3 is Defined (institutionalized) – OGC guidance is defined/confirmed as a standard business process.

For more information on the TSO maturity mark and how it can help you, please visit www.best-management-practice.com

Introduction

1

1   Introduction

There are many publications and training courses on project management. However, very little is written about project leadership. Using the search term 'project management', a random internet search brought up eight times as many entries as the term 'project leadership'. Running the same search on the website of a leading online bookseller the ratio was worse – more than 5,000 books on project management and only 134 books on project leadership.

Does this mean that leadership is less valuable than management? Certainly, the experienced project and programme managers and sponsors who were interviewed for this publication would strongly disagree. In fact, one of the reasons that this publication has been written is the frustration that many managers have with staff who can clearly 'manage' a situation but cannot 'lead' the resources that are involved.

It is easy to see why there is a bias towards management. Leadership is incredibly difficult to describe and to give examples of. It is an intangible human quality that inspires us to follow the direction set by someone else. Leadership entails moving people towards a vision of the future, trying to make sure that everyone is moving towards the same vision at roughly the same time. This involves encouragement, motivation of others, resolving disagreements and overcoming resistance.

Within a project or programme environment, leadership means influencing, persuading and controlling resources that have multiple reporting lines and varying levels of commitment to the projects. Too often, expected progress is not achieved because of numerous people-related issues such as:

- Not finishing a piece of work on time, because it was not regarded as the most important piece of work on the desk at the time
- Refusal to work with other teams or departments because of past conflicts or a general lack of cooperation amongst the participants
- Simple misunderstandings escalating into conflict because no-one checked with anyone else how their objectives contributed to the overall objectives of the project.

Although project management techniques provide a structure for planning, monitoring and controlling projects, very little is offered in terms of people management and the experiences associated with the type of matrix management that is common within projects. This publication, through the use of examples and anecdotes, looks at how common leadership activities can provide a structure for these complex issues throughout the project lifecycle.

1.1   THE AUDIENCE FOR THIS PUBLICATION

This publication is for anyone who is responsible for persuading, motivating and energizing their colleagues to get started on a piece of work, convincing them that they are heading in the right direction or encouraging them to see how their work fits into the bigger picture. The publication describes situations where the need for leadership manifests itself within a project or programme, and uses a case study to illustrate how effective leadership within this environment can be demonstrated. It will be of most use to those managers who wish to enhance their skill set and develop confidence to effectively deal with the increasing interpersonal and communication demands that arise through the organization of work into projects and programmes.

This publication forms part of a series of three publications, each highlighting a specific area of interpersonal skills demonstrated by effective project and programme managers:

- Communication skills
- Leadership skills
- Team management skills.

The intended audience for these publications is not restricted solely to those already working in project or programme management, but includes anyone who is impacted by projects within their day-to-day work. However, a basic understanding of what a project is, and the organization structure that underpins projects and programmes, has been assumed.

1.2 THE STRUCTURE OF THIS PUBLICATION

Chapter 2 defines leadership and how it applies to project and programme management. Chapter 3 explores the different leadership challenges that arise as a typical project lifecycle unfolds. The examples in this chapter are based on a self-contained project, but the ideas are valid for programmes and for the projects that form those programmes. This is a practical guide, so for each section of the lifecycle, suggestions have been made about how to undertake leadership activities, based on four common themes:

- Taking a long-range perspective
- Creating the best possible environment to ensure success
- Bringing together the right people
- Innovating and developing new approaches.

Throughout the text, you will find advice and opinions from project and programme managers and sponsors in boxes labelled 'Real world experience'. These quotes

illustrate how to implement certain ideas, and in some cases give ideas about what to avoid.

Appendix A provides advice on how to prioritize leadership activities and maintain a leadership approach whilst under the pressure of being a project or programme leader. Appendix B gives guidance on how to undertake the key leadership activities of chairing meetings and taking decisions, and gives guidance on the benefits and use of influencing skills. Appendix C discusses the appropriate choice of leadership style in relation to organizational culture.

1.3 WORKING WITHIN A PROJECT OR PROGRAMME MANAGEMENT ENVIRONMENT

A project is a temporary organization structure that is created to deliver outputs (products and services) that are justified on the basis that the benefits of having these outputs outweigh the cost of delivering them. The most obvious leader within a project environment is the project sponsor or the project executive. However, leadership responsibilities are also held by the project manager, and should also be demonstrated by anyone leading a team of specialists responsible for the creation of the project outputs.

A programme is a temporary organization structure that is created to coordinate and direct the implementation of a set of related projects and activities in order to deliver outcomes and benefits that will drive forward the achievement of an organization's strategy. The most obvious leader within a programme environment is the programme sponsor, also known as the senior responsible owner. However, the programme manager has many leadership responsibilities, including the need to lead the efforts of all the projects within the programme. In addition, programmes also have business change managers, who are responsible for leading changes within their operational environments that are necessary if the benefits of the programme are to be realized.

To save repetition throughout the text, the terms project and project management have been used to represent activities and responsibilities that take place within a project or a programme environment.

This publication introduces the key concepts and techniques of leadership within a project management environment, where the resources are not line managed by those in a project leadership role, and where the authority to implement changes brought about by the projects is held by operational managers and not project leaders.

For the purposes of this publication, the role of the project leader is referred to in a generic form, without reference to any specific project or programme management roles. However, the leadership activities that are included within the lifecycle explained in Chapter 2 incorporate the leadership responsibilities commonly associated with the roles of:

- Project sponsor
- Project executive
- Programme sponsor
- Senior responsible owner
- Project manager
- Programme manager.

The project and programme management terminology used in this publication is based on the suite of guidance developed by the Office of Government Commerce (OGC), aimed at helping organizations manage projects and programmes. Principally, the terminology has been drawn from two approaches:

- PRINCE2™
- Managing Successful Programmes (MSP™).

Terminology from these approaches is included in the glossary at the end of this publication.

Figures 1.1–1.3 provide an overview of the links between the two approaches and the lifecycle model that is used in Chapter 3.

Figure 1.1 Getting started – overview of the links between PRINCE2, MSP and the lifecycle model

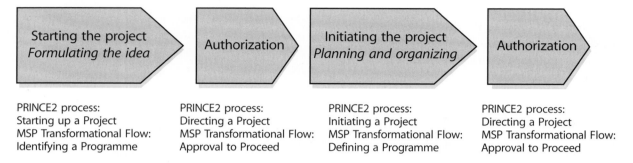

PRINCE2 process:
Starting up a Project
MSP Transformational Flow:
Identifying a Programme

PRINCE2 process:
Directing a Project
MSP Transformational Flow:
Approval to Proceed

PRINCE2 process:
Initiating a Project
MSP Transformational Flow:
Defining a Programme

PRINCE2 process:
Directing a Project
MSP Transformational Flow:
Approval to Proceed

Figure 1.2 Making progress – overview of the links between PRINCE2, MSP and the lifecycle model

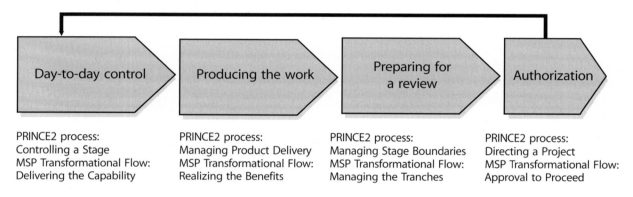

PRINCE2 process:
Controlling a Stage
MSP Transformational Flow:
Delivering the Capability

PRINCE2 process:
Managing Product Delivery
MSP Transformational Flow:
Realizing the Benefits

PRINCE2 process:
Managing Stage Boundaries
MSP Transformational Flow:
Managing the Tranches

PRINCE2 process:
Directing a Project
MSP Transformational Flow:
Approval to Proceed

Figure 1.3 Closing down – overview of the links between PRINCE2, MSP and the lifecycle model

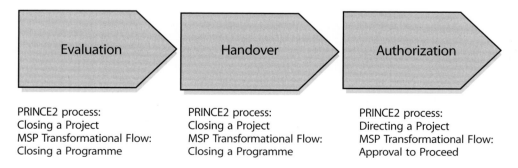

PRINCE2 process:
Closing a Project
MSP Transformational Flow:
Closing a Programme

PRINCE2 process:
Closing a Project
MSP Transformational Flow:
Closing a Programme

PRINCE2 process:
Directing a Project
MSP Transformational Flow:
Approval to Proceed

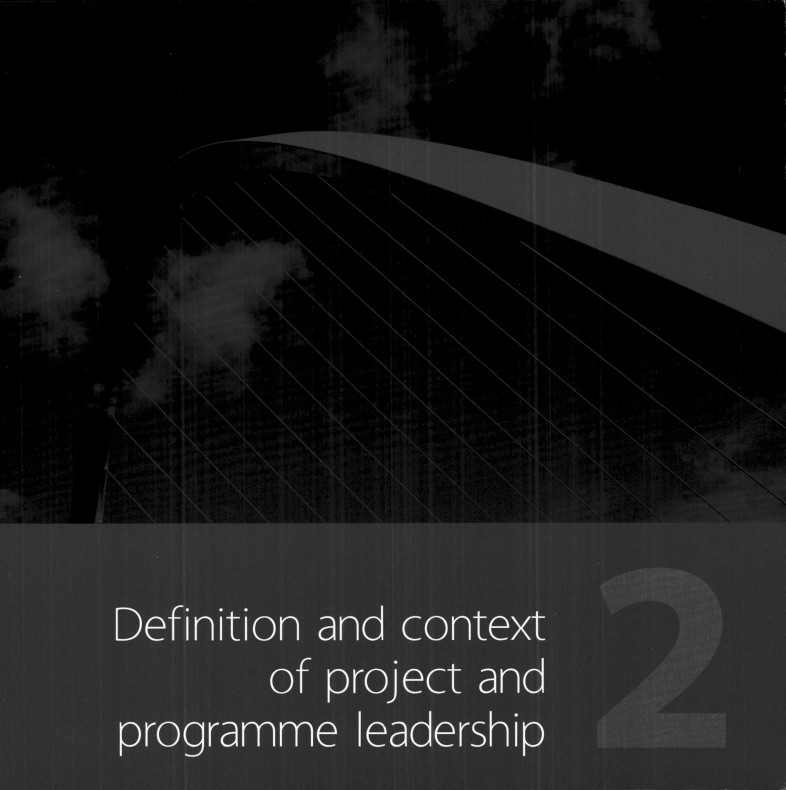

Definition and context of project and programme leadership

2

2 Definition and context of project and programme leadership

'Leadership is the ability to establish vision and direction, to influence and align others towards a common purpose, and to empower and inspire people to achieve project success. It enables the project to proceed in an environment of change and uncertainty.' (Project Management Body of Knowledge, Association for Project Management)

'Leadership is a function of knowing yourself, having a vision that is well communicated, building trust among colleagues and taking effective action to realise your own leadership potential.' (Warren Bennis, Professor of Business Administration and Founding Chairman of the Leadership Institute at the University of Southern California)

2.1 LEADERSHIP VERSUS MANAGEMENT

One of the main contributors of leadership over management is that management concentrates on the tactical, whereas leadership concentrates on the strategic. Therefore, project leadership contributes to setting the direction and ensuring the viability of what is being undertaken whilst project management ensures that products and services produced by the project are capable of meeting a business need. Leadership has to define what that business need is and constantly check that this business need still exists (Table 2.1).

Table 2.1 Comparison of management and leadership attributes

Management	Leadership
Administers	Directs
Concentrates on project administration, including focus on reports being delivered on time and in the correct format, ensuring plans are always up to date	Looks for the essence of the information from the reports
Accepts current constraints	Challenges current constraints
Works within the existing organizational structures and procedures	Identifies any problems with existing structures and procedures and suggests alternatives
Relies on control	Inspires trust
Uses authority conferred by job title and position in the organization to issue instructions and set deadlines to get the job done	Uses ability to persuade, energize and motivate, and ensures the best possible environment is created to get the job done
Concerned with resources	Concerned with reasons
Concentrates on timeframe, budget and available resources within which the project must deliver	Concentrates on reasons for existence of the project and benefits that the project will deliver

In summary, project leadership ensures that the right things are being done, whilst project management ensures that things are being done in the right way. Therefore, project management is much more concerned with the processes by which the project runs day to day, whilst project leadership concentrates on what those processes are leading to, and whether they are what is required. Project leadership requires information from a range of sources external to the project, whilst the information requirements for project management are more heavily weighted towards analysis of actual project performance against plan.

This publication has been based firmly on the belief that leaders are not born, they can be made. Leadership skills, competencies and even characteristics can be learnt, given the right environment and exposure to training and support.

A leader has to establish whom they will lead and the environment in which they will lead. During the lifecycle of a project, those who need to be led will change (Figure 2.1). To get the project off the ground, effort should be concentrated on those most immediately involved, including the project team and those who will decide the objectives, scope, funding and timetable for the project. As the project nears completion, the opposite could be said to be true – the work of the project team comes to an end, and the implementation activities usually undertaken by operational staff expected to use and operate the products of the project increase. Therefore, the project leader will be spending more time with this group, and will need to establish themselves as a leader of this effort, even though they are not their operational manager.

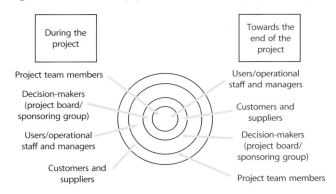

Figure 2.1 Leadership priorities over the project lifecycle

During the project

Towards the end of the project

Project team members
Decision-makers (project board/ sponsoring group)
Users/operational staff and managers
Customers and suppliers

Users/operational staff and managers
Customers and suppliers
Decision-makers (project board/ sponsoring group)
Project team members

2.2 LEADERSHIP BEHAVIOURS

Leaders need to inspire people to become followers. The ability to inspire is directly connected to the behaviours that the leader displays. Whilst an individual cannot become a different person, it is possible to increase the demonstration of certain behaviours that embody effective leadership including:

- Being motivated by goals and a vision of a better future
- Having an open mind
- Using a strong sense of political awareness
- Being tolerant of ambiguity and uncertainty
- Encouraging dissent and challenge
- Having a consistent manner
- Displaying emotional restraint
- Having a sense of self-worth
- Having the confidence to work with others more qualified and experienced than themselves.

These behaviours enable a person to become an effective leader by ensuring that they engage with people on an emotional and not just a logical basis. Essentially, in order to become a follower, a person must feel that the leader understands and shares their core values and beliefs. The leader cannot make this link unless they take action to

Figure 2.2 Leadership competencies

Taking a long-range perspective	Creating the best possible environment to ensure success
• Motivated by goals and a vision of a better future • Using a strong sense of political awareness • Being tolerant of ambiguity and uncertainty	• Having an open mind • Encouraging dissent and challenge • Having a consistent manner • Displaying emotional restraint • Having a sense of self-worth
• Having an open mind • Having a consistent manner • Displaying emotional restraint • Having a sense of self-worth • Having the humility to work with others more qualified and experienced than themselves	• Having an open mind • Being motivated by goals and a vision of a better future • Having the humility to work with others more qualified and experienced than themselves
Bringing together the right people	Innovating and developing new approaches

discover what these values are, and behave empathetically towards them.

The values that are held by those involved in project and programme management will affect every aspect of the lifecycle. For example:

■ Strong ethical values regarding the difference between lying, i.e. deliberately providing false information, and withholding the truth will impact on the contents of progress reports, and the tone in which progress information, risks and issues are presented to decision-makers.

■ Values connected to what constitutes a fair day's work will impact on the estimating of task durations and the amount of work that can be successfully delegated to the project team.

■ Values that underpin a person's view of being responsible for something will guide how much initiative they display when carrying out tasks and finding solutions for problems.

The ability to demonstrate these behaviours is linked to the ability to succeed in the four core leadership competencies (Figure 2.2) that are demonstrated throughout the lifecycle of a project.

2.3 LEADERSHIP ACTIVITIES REQUIRED IN A PROJECT

Taking a long-range perspective

Leaders must understand the widest possible context of any effort that they are leading. This means understanding how the project or programme will help to achieve the better future outlined in the strategy and by direction of the organization as a whole. The leader must also understand the political concerns that the project or programme raises and develop an awareness of how it is perceived outside the team responsible for its delivery, so that any negative views can be positively influenced.

For those responsible for day-to-day project leadership, there must be an understanding of how the successful delivery of new products and services that the organization does not currently possess will affect the capability of the departments or functions that will come to own these deliverables.

For those responsible for leading the sponsorship of the project, there must be an understanding of how this new capability affects any power bases within the organization, and therefore who the perceived winners and losers are, as this will affect the membership of the project board and the political support that the project receives throughout its lifecycle.

For those responsible for shepherding a programme through its lifecycle, there must be an understanding of how the successful completion will impact on the stakeholders in terms of how they perceive the organization and how they interact with the organization.

Creating the best possible environment to ensure success

Leaders must create an environment where views and opinions can be raised without fear of censure. Leaders must encourage dissent and challenge, and have the confidence and emotional restraint for this to happen. Trust must be placed in the project team members, so that they feel empowered to undertake their role.

This requires the leader to be willing to share their thoughts and explain their reasoning, which enables team members to develop an understanding of the context of

what they are being asked to do. Leaders need to ensure that what they say they will do and what they actually do is consistent, so that others feel they can be trusted.

For those responsible for day-to-day project leadership the leader creates an environment in which the project team, and to some extent the operational staff who are impacted by the project, can freely exchange ideas and debate possible solutions.

For those responsible for leading the sponsorship of the project, respect must be shown by all those willing to support the project, and to those who challenge it.

In a programme, there is a need for the leader to widen their responsibility to ensure that all stakeholders are engaged in a sympathetic and helpful manner, where the flow of information is truly two-way.

Bringing together the right people

There is a need to ensure that those given specific roles within the project are appropriately skilled and experienced and are able to use their skills, through delegation of authority and empowering staff to take responsibility for their actions. The leader must develop an understanding of the way in which different personalities address their work, and the strengths and weaknesses of everyone involved in the project, including themselves, and be open minded enough to realize that their solution is not the only solution.

For those responsible for day-to-day project leadership, bringing together the right people extends to the project team and users taking part in requirements definition and user testing. In a programme, the range of people involved and impacted on is much wider, and there is a need to build many more alliances and networks to ensure information flows between them.

For those responsible for leading the sponsorship of the project, assessment of strengths, weaknesses and levels of experience will be tempered by levels of authority and political support. The leader must be aware of how these factors have influenced the membership of the project board and the level of support that exists for the project.

For those responsible for shepherding the programme through its lifecycle, there is a responsibility to bring together and engage with the widest possible range of stakeholders to ensure that all views are heard and addressed.

Innovating and developing new approaches

Leaders understand the specifics of their environment, and will develop new approaches to suit their requirements, rather than being constrained by and replicating what has gone before. Innovation is an attitude of openness to new ideas and a willingness to apply lateral thinking to overcome challenges. The leader must create an environment that supports individual, team and organizational learning and development. Everyone involved in the project must be encouraged to develop the attitude of 'How can we improve this?'.

Innovation goes hand in hand with projects and programmes because both are vehicles for delivering new products, services and capability into the organization. Therefore, as a minimum, the leader must encourage the development of new ways of working and new ways of thinking that fully utilize what has been created. When an organization applies methods such as PRINCE2 or MSP to its projects and programmes, leaders can sometimes feel constrained from developing new ways of working within the project teams, because the structure and order of the work has already been defined by the method. However, an effective leader must always look for the opportunity to develop new alliances, to share information in new and more relevant ways, and to encourage the development of new relationships that lead to new ideas.

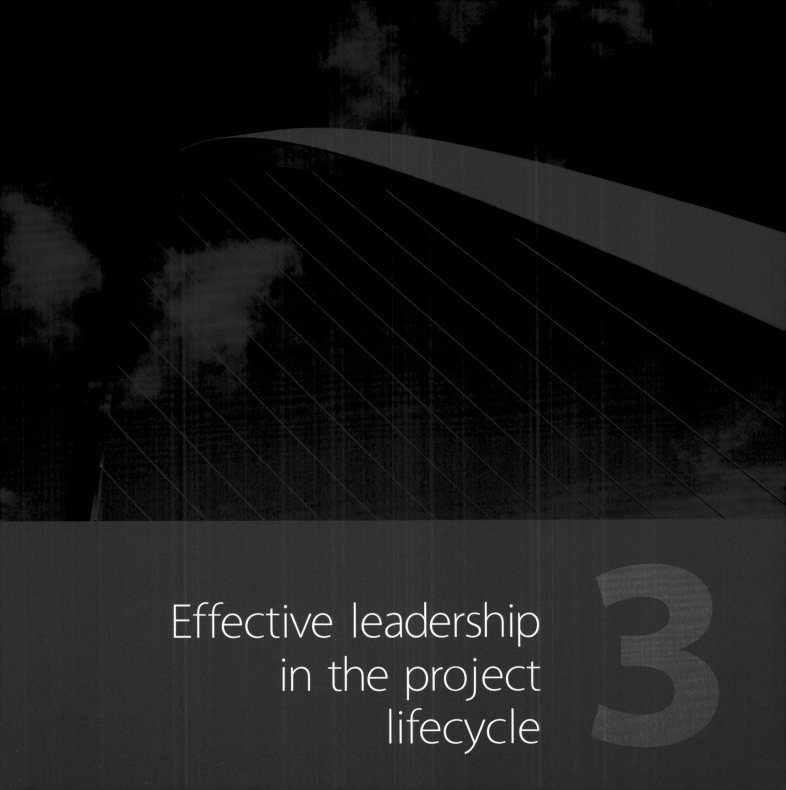

Effective leadership in the project lifecycle

3

3 Effective leadership in the project lifecycle

This chapter explains how leadership skills are applied in each step of the project lifecycle. The leadership challenges and solutions described are drawn from interviews with many people in project leadership roles. The descriptions of the different facets of leadership have been illustrated with a case study based on a typical project whose characteristics are representative of a range of internal projects undertaken within organizations. The text is complemented by quotes from the interviewees, presented as 'Real world experience'.

Case study: the 'Info~U~Want' project

Info~U~Want is a medium-sized research agency that has recently completed a strategic review of its operations, drawing the conclusion that to meet its growth targets it needs to expand its product range and serve a wider customer base than is currently the case. It is now halfway through the year, and the directors of each department within the organization have been tasked with identifying ways in which the strategic objectives can be met. There are four directors, who form the senior management team (SMT) and they report to the board of directors (Figure 3.1).

Figure 3.1 Structure of the Info~U~Want research agency

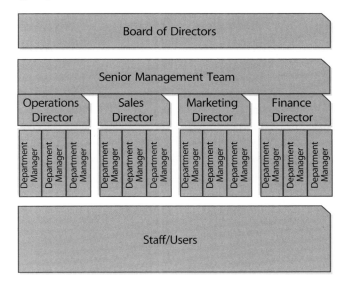

A new initiative: unified document management

The operations director takes responsibility for ensuring that the core operating processes of the organization can support the development of new products and increased sales to a wider customer base. As a result of the strategic review, the operations director has concluded that the organization cannot effectively develop its product range without first developing an accurate understanding of all the research material the organization owns and manages. The structure that currently exists makes it difficult to access material managed by a department other than the one in which a staff member is working, and the operations director suspects that this leads to a lot of duplication, as well as an incomplete picture of the capability of the organization.

The operations director has had the idea of developing a single unified document management system as the best way to contribute to the successful delivery of the organization's strategic objectives.

Project or programme?

Using the definition of a project given in Chapter 1, this initiative could be run as a single project, with a project manager reporting directly to the operations director, who takes the role of project sponsor or project executive (Figure 3.2). However, this initiative could equally be run as a programme, where there is a programme manager reporting to the operations director, who takes the role of programme sponsor or senior responsible owner. In this case, individual projects would be run within each of the departments, with a project manager to run each project and a business change manager to implement the new systems and procedures (Figure 3.3).

Figure 3.2 Running the new initiative as a project

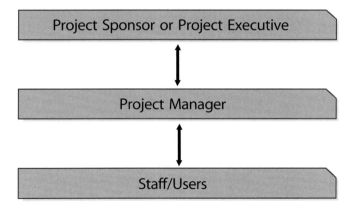

Figure 3.3 Running the new initiative as a programme

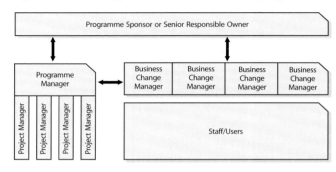

Leadership challenges within the initiative

Whether the initiative is run as a project or a programme, there are several leadership challenges that need to be addressed by the project or programme manager, and the project or programme sponsor:

- The project is objected to by many of the departmental managers because they feel that their departments already have a working system and they will see no benefits to all the work involved in migration of individual file structures and document naming conventions to a single company-wide structure.
- Managers within each department feel strongly that their approach to document management is the best approach and other managers cannot see the point of the project as it will take valuable time and get in the way of creating new products.
- The project is based on efficiency and internal reorganization, which means that it is not directly tied to the creation of revenue (which might provide it with management support and buy-in) and it is sorting out an issue that is not regulated or licensed (so there is no regulatory imperative to undertake the project).

Although the operations director is a member of the SMT there is still the need for a great deal of cooperation between other directors and their direct reports if this project is to be successful. In their role as sponsor, the operations director will need to lead the project or programme through the decision-making process of the SMT and the board of directors.

3.1 GETTING STARTED – STARTING THE PROJECT

The project will be triggered by a mandate from senior management, which outlines the idea for the project and may also indicate the constraints within which the project must deliver, such as the timeframe or expected budget. The idea for the project will be based on the need to deliver the strategy and goals of the organization. The scope and objectives of the project will be captured in a brief, which will describe the capability that the organization wishes to create as a result of the project, and the benefits of having this capability.

Decisions will need to be taken on how the project will be undertaken, either by using in-house staff, or by hiring supplier organizations or consultants, and this will impact on the reporting lines and levels of authority given to each role within the organization structure. As these decisions are being taken so early in the project lifecycle, participants may not be appointed to their roles until the project has been formally authorized.

Leadership activities required when formulating the idea for a project

■ Identify how the project will contribute to delivering the better future that is outlined by the strategy and objectives of the organization

■ Develop an environment where the idea for the project can be challenged and discussed without fear of censure or criticism.

Taking a long-range perspective

When formulating the idea for a project or programme, the leader often has to develop an idea that has been passed from senior management. To lead the project or programme through its lifecycle to successful conclusion, the leader needs to understand the background to the idea and develop the information into a guiding vision that aligns the direction of the project or programme in terms of the strategic direction of the organization.

> **Real world experience**
> 'I need to believe in it and to do that I need to understand it. So I will ask a lot of "dumb" questions at the start of the project until I am clear. After all, the sponsor might know what they want, but when I start managing the project, I become its face, and people can spot fake belief and enthusiasm from 50 paces.'

Case study: implications for Info~U~Want

The project vision: In this example, is the document management system an essential structure upon which the growth plans of Info~U~Want can be based? By having this system in place, can the organization leverage economies of scale from existing work? To effectively lead this project, the operations director will need to put forward a compelling reason that can be used to overcome the opposition of those managers who believe it will waste time or get in the way of new products. The leader must understand how this contributes to the strategic direction of the organization, and build a vision of how the future will look when the project objectives have been achieved (Figure 3.4).

The project is likely to be seen by many operational managers as a cost to the business with very few

Figure 3.4 Project vision

This vision is short, providing a high-level description of the project without going too deep into the detail of what exactly will be produced, when and by whom

'The project will develop a single, unified document management system.'

'The ability of the organization to develop new products within every department is enhanced by clear visibility of what products the organization already has, who owns them, who created them, and on what earlier versions of products they were based.'

'This information is accessible to all, minimizing the risk of duplication of effort and encouraging cross-departmental development and ideas generation.'

Features of the system are clearly set out, indicating that the project is well understood by those responsible for it

The benefits are an important way for individuals to establish that their contribution to the project will be seen in measurable improvements to the organization, and the aspirational statements help staff to feel motivated to take part

financial benefits. This may lead to a lack of support or prioritization of the project work during the life of the project. To overcome this, the leader must present a strong Business Case for the project, clearly showing its links to future revenue generation by providing the organization with a lower cost base for future product development.

In a programme environment, the business change manager will be responsible for the identification of these benefits and establishing a compelling vision of the operational benefits that operational staff and managers wish to enjoy. For example, at Info~U~Want, the business change manager would lead the dissenting managers through all the costs of developing a new research product using the current procedures and then show how many of these costs were eradicated as a result of

accessing information quickly and accurately via the new document management system.

Winning over dissenters: The ability of the leader to lead dissenters from resistance to support is impacted by the level of empathy that the leader has with the situation which the dissenters are experiencing. It might be difficult for a programme or project manager with no experience of creating research products at Info~U~Want to demonstrate empathy with the situation. A leader drawn from within the operation can use their own experiences as 'evidence' of the problems, which gives them credibility with their audience when they then present the solution, i.e. the new document management system.

However, not all leaders will have direct experience of the situation through which they are trying to lead people, but they are still strong leaders. This is because they use

Figure 3.5 Building the case for a new document management system at Info~U~Want

'Difficult' and 'frustrating' were words that were used repeatedly by those the leader talked to	I was talking to James last night, and he told me what a difficult and frustrating time he is having with new product development.
Description of the problem	He believes that the development time for each research assignment is much longer than the sales department realizes, and that they are giving unrealistic deadlines to the clients. This is because, as you know, every time there is a request for a new piece of research, we have to start from scratch, as it takes a long time to find old pieces of work on the same subject, and even if they can be found, there is often a fight within our own company about ownership of the material.
'Our own company' shows the leader as 'one of the group'	Last month, James found that the work that took him two weeks to put together had already been done by the EMEA department.
Impact of the problem	There is no organization-wide catalogue of existing products and whilst we have a great list within our department, it only goes back as far as last summer, as the temp we hired to do the indexing was with us for only three months.
	We are getting a reputation with sales of being slow and lazy when we are actually working longer hours. James was in the office until 8.30pm again last night, and I know a number of you have been doing similar hours, and working at weekends as well.
Description of the solution	The new document management system will provide a full company index of existing products and the procedures associated with its use will resolve the current constraints over ownership.
Impact of the solution	Requests for new pieces of research will now begin with an automatic search of the database for similar, recent products and it will become common practice to enhance existing material rather than always create from new each time, which will halve the development time, and put it back in line with the timeframe that sales are selling to our customers.

the experiences of others and weave them into a story that they narrate for their audience of potential followers. The effectiveness of the story is increased by using the exact words and phrases that have been told to them to create a logical structure that establishes a clear time and place in which the story takes place:

- Description of the problem: impact of problem, i.e. cost to the organization expressed in terms of the 'pain' experienced by the audience
- Description of the solution: impact of solution, i.e. the benefits to the organization in terms of the improvements that the audience will experience.

At Info~U~Want, the leader of the project might tell the story depicted in Figure 3.5.

Fitting the project within the organization's strategy: It is essential that those responsible for leading the sponsorship of projects and programmes develop a mechanism that will allow them to monitor changes to the strategic direction of the organization, so that any impact on the project or programme can be identified and acted on if necessary. The leader will need to demonstrate a strong sense of political awareness to track who can influence strategy, and what their view of the world will do to the direction of the organization over time.

Need for identifying high-level goals: In leading a programme, it is not always possible to identify all of the tangible deliverables that will result from the successful delivery of the programme this early in its lifecycle. Therefore, the leader may need to identify the high-level goals that the programme will achieve and generate support and commitment to these instead of a list of specific deliverables.

High-level goals can sometimes be harder for people to engage with because there is no actual product or service to endorse. However, the leader can link the high-level goals to the values that are important to staff within the organization, which makes it easier to engage with them and support them. For example, Info~U~Want has a culture of empowerment where staff are encouraged to continually develop their role and seek out additional responsibilities. This is supported by a culture of continuous learning and development where training and the development of new skills is actively encouraged. In this case, the leader could link the development of file sharing across departments to the concept of widening the remit of each researcher to be responsible for enhancing the quality of research materials across the organization and not just across their own department. The adoption of a new document management system gives staff the chance to deepen their IT skills.

Creating the best possible environment to ensure success

When the idea for a project is still being defined, it is important that the leader creates an environment where all involved feel able to raise their concerns, add ideas and challenge the need for the project.

This is an essential step in building buy-in and support. This support will not develop if the leader presents the project to all those impacted by it, without allowing these discussions to take place. The leader must be open minded, and at times will need to display emotional restraint. For example, when suggestions about the scope of the project expand to include work that the project leader thinks is unnecessary, the leader must not react negatively but should instead seek to discover why this scope is being suggested. Sometimes the ideas behind a project evolve because managers see the project as a vehicle for achieving some or all of their objectives, whether or not they are connected to the project. The leader must investigate first; understand the underlying 'opportunism' before developing arguments to explain why that particular scope for the project is unacceptable.

> **Real world experience**
> 'Leadership is about showing strength and confidence. I think my colleagues believe that listening is a sign of weakness because it signals uncertainty about the way forward. I think it shows strength because it says I am willing to do this work with you, and not do it to you.'

Case study: winning universal support

At Info~U~Want, there is a great deal of opposition from departmental managers to the project. In this case, the leader will have to demonstrate that they are an 'honest broker'. This means clarifying in detail exactly where the managers believe the project is going over old ground, and developing a set of criteria for identifying the best approach for the organization, rather than being seen to 'play favourites' by adopting an existing solution from one of the departments, or deciding to ignore everything that has gone on before and developing a completely new solution.

These criteria will need to be clear to everyone and consistently applied to each idea or possible solution. At this stage in the project lifecycle the leader must ensure that the appropriate idea is formulated; therefore facilitating the exchange of information between all of the interested parties is of paramount importance. This can only be achieved if there is a trust between those parties and the project leader.

Ultimately, the project leader will need to identify possible solutions and present these to senior management, as it is they who have the authority to make the decisions. Overall, this can be a lengthy process, involving many conversations and follow-up meetings (Figure 3.6). Although the figure shows the position of the project manager between the project stakeholders and the project sponsor, the same 'honest broker' situation occurs within programme management, where the programme manager has to mediate between the programme stakeholders and the sponsoring group.

Figure 3.6 The project leader as the 'honest broker'

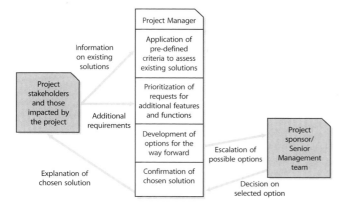

During this process, the leader must demonstrate excellent judgement and reasoning skills to be able to navigate through the ideas that are being presented by the various stakeholders, drawing together the conflicting ideas and demands until an agreed solution is designed. This also requires confidence and decisiveness, as some objectives will need to be dropped and others given a lower priority than some stakeholders would prefer.

Leaders will find it helpful to keep records of all the reasons behind the decisions that are taken at this time, as one of their key roles will be to explain the situation in such a way that all stakeholders feel that they can give the project or programme their support, even if their own agenda has not been included.

3.2   GETTING STARTED – AUTHORIZATION

Once the idea for the project has been formulated, the leader will need to guide the project through its first official authorization, when the decision-makers endorse the initial Business Case for the project, and confirm that they believe the idea has merit and is viable.

Leadership activities required when authorizing the idea for a project

- Understand the long-term implications for the organization of successfully delivering this project
- Bring together the most appropriate resources to sponsor and champion the project throughout its life.

Whilst the leader is not the only decision-maker in this instance, the leader has to ensure that the view that the decision-makers have of the potential project is positive, has a strong direction and has commitment from across the organization. Therefore, the leader has to demonstrate that there are already 'followers' who will follow the leader in the delivery of the project. The leader needs to understand the level of support for the idea, and the conversations, meetings and analysis which have gone on behind the scenes prior to the production of the project mandate.

Taking a long-range perspective

To gain the support of the project board, the leader responsible for leading the sponsorship of the project must demonstrate that they have considered the 'bigger picture'. They must show that the scope of the project – illustrated by the vision statement – is neither too narrow that it wastes opportunities to achieve, nor too ambitious that it runs the risk of having too many interfaces with other organizational initiatives and so could get bogged down. The leader must also consider the power of highlighting the implications of not carrying out the project, as outlining the problems associated with 'staying as we are' can create a powerful desire to commit to the project.

Case study: the project within the bigger picture

The long-range perspective of Info~U~Want is to expand its product range and serve a wider customer base. The operations director must demonstrate how successful completion of the document management project will 'lead' Info~U~Want to achieving this objective. This will involve outlining how the organization will have a greater understanding of its own product range, past and present, and how it can more effectively share information across departments. The operations director should explain the effects in terms of cost and time of continuing to have 'silos' of information that are often duplicated across a growing business.

Bringing together the right people

The leader has to establish the relevant board that will form the decision-making group for the life of the project. For this board to function effectively, there must be a balance between colleagues who can effectively support each other and still bring sufficient challenge and rigour to the decision-making process.

Leadership is about knowing and applying the principles of creating an effective project board – who should be invited onto this board and who should be left out. A project board should include representatives from the user and the supplier communities who have sufficient authority to be the decision-makers for the project. Without this level of authority, there will be the constant need to refer discussions from the project board back to more senior managers, which will lead to delays and confusion.

Thus the leader must scan the environment for political alliances, power bases and hidden agendas that may have an effect on the orientation of the board. For example, the leader should ask themselves the following questions:

- Are there managers who always back up each other and will automatically agree with any decision that the other one takes?
- Are there managers who are targeting the same promotion and are therefore keen to become involved in the project as a way of raising their profile?
- Are there managers who will fight the project because they have been promoting an alternative way forward and do not want to lose face?

In bringing together the right people, leaders must not be naïve in assessing interpersonal relationships and the forces that drive them.

For those responsible for shepherding a programme through its lifecycle, this authorization stage provides an opportunity to engage with many of the most powerful stakeholders who form the sponsoring group for the programme.

> **Real world experience**
>
> 'I create a list of all the people who are likely to oppose the project and why they will oppose it. Even though I might not be able to change their minds, remembering why they are opposed gives me confidence – it's not my failure, it's just that they have a different opinion that should be acknowledged and given some respect.'

Case study: groundwork required before setting up the project board

At Info~U~Want, the project will enhance cross-departmental working by making knowledge about the ownership of products more open to those outside the department that originally created it. Therefore, the project leader will need to consider which senior managers (potential members of the board) actively support this open agenda, and which of them are likely to oppose it, albeit in an indirect manner.

If one unified method of document management is to be developed across the organization, are there alliances between departments that will be strengthened or weakened by the project? How will this affect the membership of the board?

The project leader also has to consider possible resentment of the project by those departments that believe that in the past they have been affected by projects indirectly but not consulted or involved directly. The operations director should try to find out if the audit department is likely to be affected by the openness of the new world created by the project – for example, in the way in which internal audits and reviews on the internal operation of the company can be carried out. If the project board only involves 'old favourites', resentment can build up.

It is not easy for one person to understand all of the alliances that exist within an organization, so a project leader should consult heavily about the membership of the newly formed project board, and can use this time as an opportunity to continue scanning the environment for pockets of support or resistance that will affect the progress of the project once it is up and running.

> **Real world experience**
>
> 'Leadership is sometimes about staying firm and not backing down. Cost cutting often means being assigned a smaller project team than I need, or being given junior staff for complex, high-risk projects. My leadership role is to speak up on behalf of everyone involved and explain what this really means – delays, less of an ability to get the right solution first time, etc.'

3.3 GETTING STARTED – INITIATING THE PROJECT

Once the high-level scope of a project has been agreed, there is a need to plan the work, assign resources and prepare the project environment, including access to office space, IT systems and other resources.

Planning will identify the activities that will need to be undertaken to develop the required products or services and the resources needed to carry them out. Therefore, the project leader needs to understand the operational priorities that exist within the organization and how this might affect resource availability. Although a decision on how the project is to be approached will have been taken as the idea was developed in starting the project, questions must be asked about the true capability of the firm to develop products in-house, or the ability and willingness of the organization to work with outside suppliers.

Leadership activities required when initiating a project

■ Develop an environment where people want to become involved and share their information and knowledge

■ Bring together the right people to ensure the integrity and accuracy of the plans and estimates that will form the Project Plan.

Creating the best possible environment to ensure success

A great deal of project effort, especially in the early part of the lifecycle, relies on the ability of the leader to participate, as many of the project roles have not yet been formally appointed because the project has not been fully authorized. In order to influence those with knowledge, skills and information to participate in the planning of the project, the leader must use their emotional intelligence to assess the interests and driving forces of those whose help is needed.

The decision that everyone takes before becoming involved in a new initiative is to ask themselves the question 'What's in it for me?'. The leader needs to understand a number of factors so that they can tailor the answer to this question to each participant, such as:

■ The culture of the organization – is cross-departmental information sharing the expected norm or is there a more closed, 'silo' based mentality?

■ Does the culture reward those who 'go the extra mile' or is involvement in activities outside the job description seen as 'pushy' and 'driven'?

■ Is there freedom to reward worthwhile contributions with the offer of project roles?

■ Is praise for creative thinking seen as genuine or dismissed as sycophancy?

■ Is there a history of honouring contributions with at least a name check when projects are successful?

Bringing together the right people

The person responsible for day-to-day leadership of a project does not necessarily have specialist knowledge about the products and services being created, nor do they need to be able to plan every activity in the project. They must have the ability to recognize the value that others can offer, and to involve those more qualified and experienced than themselves, and this is especially important when leading a programme in which the scope of the specialist work can be wide ranging.

The leader should involve project team members and operational staff to identify the tasks that must be included in the plan, and the duration and required resources for these tasks. The leader must use their communication skills to build networks and alliances across the team to create a collaborative environment, where team members are prepared to speak up and share their knowledge and ideas. Project team members will be more committed to the desired outcome as they have been a part of deciding that outcome. Solutions are likely to be more robust than those created under pressure, as there has been more discussion, greater exchange of information and a willingness to investigate new ideas.

It is not always possible to identify all of the resources needed for this task immediately, as a conversation with one specialist can lead to the identification of other areas of work that will need to be included. The leader will need to create a picture of the resources that they feel are essential for the planning activities, and then be prepared to build on this as the process unfolds. One technique that many leaders use is the creation of a network diagram (Figure 3.7).

Figure 3.7 An example network diagram

Role of third-party suppliers

Some organizations work very well with third-party suppliers, with an ability to share information, share staff and develop ideas collaboratively. Other organizations have strong internal processes and systems, which third-party suppliers struggle to adapt to, in an environment where there is limited support from the organization itself to help.

The leader will need to assess the culture of the organization against these points but will also need to consider their own ability. Confidence and a willingness to listen and be flexible are three of the qualities required by the leader in working with third-party organizations and the success of new ways of working will depend on this skill level of the leader.

Confidence is a mixture of self-confidence and 'technical' confidence – in this case, knowledge of the capabilities, limitations and past history with the supplier, their products and services and knowledge of the requirements of the project or programme.

Case study: identifying resources at Info~U~Want

The leader of the Info~U~Want project, the operations director, needs to build a picture of resources based on the different conversations that they have had with staff within Info~U~Want as well as with other experts in the field of document management.

To bring together the right people to construct the plans and develop the approach to the project, the leader must retain an open mind about who the appropriate resources might be. This is an opportunity to develop strategic alliances and partnerships with other projects or teams within the organization, and other organizations including suppliers, customers and competitors. Keeping an open mind enables the leader to listen to the views of all of these parties.

Listening skills

Willingness to listen needs to be backed up by excellent listening skills. This involves three steps (Figure 3.8):

- Hearing what has been said, and not drifting off and thinking up the next question whilst the other person is still talking
- Respecting what you are being told by not speaking over the other person, or cutting them off before they have finished speaking
- Understanding what has been said, by replaying parts of the conversation as you have understood it, and asking the other person if this is what they meant.

Figure 3.8 Steps involved in listening effectively

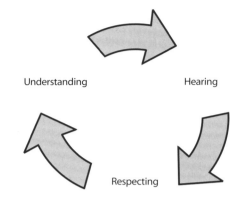

Understanding   Hearing

Respecting

Innovating and developing new approaches

The ability to be flexible is directly related to the level of understanding the leader has about the priorities and key objectives of the work involved. The leader can allow enhancements, amendments, replanning and rescheduling of work with the supplier, up to the point at which it impacts on the priorities or key objectives of the programme. As long as this point is known, the leader can demonstrate flexibility so that the customer organization and the supplier can achieve 'win-win' situations.

3.4   GETTING STARTED – AUTHORIZATION

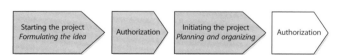

At this point, the Project Plan will be presented to the decision-makers for endorsement, which may include the formal assignment of operational resources, or the agreement to contract terms for external resources.

Leadership activities required when authorizing a project

- Understand and accept the long-range implications of committing to this project instead of other initiatives that the organization could undertake
- Create an environment where those responsible for taking decisions about the viability of the project and those authorizing the existence of the project can have faith in the information being presented to them.

Taking a long-range perspective

When presenting to the project board, the person responsible for leading the day-to-day efforts of a project must demonstrate that all aspects of the plan have been considered. For example, explain that the use of internal resources does not clash with the need to meet operational deadlines, or that the 'go live' dates for new systems and procedures do not occur at the same time as other major changes within the organization.

At authorization of any part of the project, the project leader must demonstrate their understanding of the purpose of the activities rather than presenting the details of every task. Therefore, the project leader must look beyond the detail of the plan and understand its implications for other initiatives and objectives that the organization is trying to achieve.

Case study: implications for Info~U~Want

The project leader would need to demonstrate that the implementation of the new document management system would take place soon enough to be the basis for cooperation in new product development.

Setting the limits of certainty in the projections

In leading the sponsorship of the project or programme, the leader will need to demonstrate tolerance of uncertainty and ambiguity as the plans are estimates and the information will only become more definite as the work progresses (Figure 3.9).

Figure 3.9 Certainty and the long-range perspective

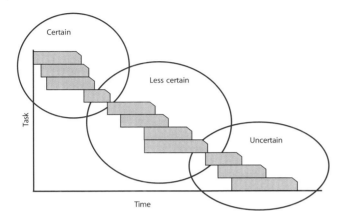

For example, the next stage of the project or the next tranche of the programme contains activities with clear estimates of the time and cost involved. However, estimates for activities in later stages or tranches are based on guesswork as the data needed to clarify them is not yet available. The leader can commit in detail to the next stage or tranche but can only authorize in principle the later work. This process runs throughout the project or programme lifecycle as accurate data becomes available. However, it is for the leader to choose when that boundary between certainty and uncertainty is reached, and only commit up to that point.

For example, the leader can assess the information that is presented to them by asking key questions:

■ How many parties have been consulted in the time and cost estimates for these activities?
■ What are the dependencies between these activities?
■ On what basis have the dependencies been identified?
■ What scheduling assumptions have been applied to create the plan, including the number of hours assumed to form a 'normal' working day?

■ What assumptions have been made about the costs included in the plan, e.g. assumed 5% increase in costs on last year, or 20% cost increase due to exchange rate fluctuations?
■ What risks have been identified in carrying out the work set out in the plan?
■ What are the reasons for the inclusion of certain activities, or the exclusion of other activities?

Creating the best possible environment to ensure success

Those responsible for taking decisions about the project must have faith in the information being presented to them. The person responsible for leading the project day to day needs to develop a working relationship that bridges the gap between the project board, which needs brevity and summary level information, and the project team and operational staff, who require detailed information and projections so that they can undertake the work and assess the level of change that will be required in their area of operation.

This working relationship is based on trust, which develops over time. However, there are a number of behaviours that the leader should demonstrate to encourage trust to develop:

■ Integrity and honesty of the information being presented: for example, authorization of the project at this point in its lifecycle means a real commitment of resources. Therefore, if there are any reasons why the project should not go ahead, the project leader has to be strong enough to clarify what these are, and offer solutions so that this commitment can be given.
■ Open minded enough to recognize that there are other paths to achieving project success, but confident enough to explain why the plan being submitted for authorization is the right one: for example, presenting all of the resourcing options that were considered

before recommending that a contract be given to external suppliers.

■ Judgement and political awareness: show an understanding of the difference between what is interesting and what is important, so that decision-makers are not presented with an overwhelming amount of information from which they are supposed to sift out the relevant pieces.

■ Recognizing the value that others more qualified and experienced than themselves can offer to the project or programme: for example, the leader involves experts and specialists who may be able to explain key aspects of the plan to the decision-makers in the most compelling way. This gives the decision-makers an opportunity to assess the quality of those in the project team as well as enabling them to gain an in-depth understanding about the project, and increasing their commitment to it.

Case study: demonstrating integrity in the face of opposition

At Info~U~Want, the departmental managers object to the document management project as they feel they already have a working system. The decision-makers will want reassurance that the project leader understands these objections, has discussed them with the managers and can clarify why a new system is needed. The leader will need to demonstrate their integrity – that vital arguments as to why this system is not needed have not been hidden or dismissed without basis, and that they have been open minded enough to consider how the strategic direction of the organization could be achieved by other means. The leader should be prepared to demonstrate their political awareness by providing a review of those most in favour and those most against the project, and how those most likely to resist it can be persuaded of its merits.

3.5 MAKING PROGRESS – DAY-TO-DAY CONTROL

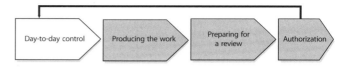

Once a project has been authorized, effort moves from establishing the environment in which the project can operate, to undertaking day-to-day project activities including development of the products and services to be produced by the project, and the monitoring and reporting of progress.

It is essential that the work delivers products and services that will meet the quality expectations and contain all the features and functions required by those who are expected to implement and adopt them.

Leadership activities required during day-to-day control of a project

■ Bring together the right people to work on the project
■ Innovate ways of working together to improve and enhance the way in which projects have been delivered in the past.

Bringing together the right people

Having the confidence to seek out and employ the right people and not just the people who are available is essential to successful project leadership. Therefore, the leader cannot simply accept the status quo. If the right people are not available then the leader will need to explain the consequences of using unskilled resources:

■ Activities take longer and are prone to more errors, pushing out the project end date
■ Incorrect solutions are selected and implemented because of a lack of knowledge of more technical approaches

■ The proportion of time taken by the leader in day-to-day project management overshadows other activities such as quality reviews, stakeholder engagement activities and development of links between the project and the delivery of the organization's strategy.

At the same time, the leader must establish support from the operational units to make staff available or get further funding to enable the project to employ the specialists that it requires.

Projects often rely on the assignment of resources from those departments and functions most impacted by the project, where assignment results from availability rather than from an assessment of the skills required. Therefore, leading project resources often requires an honest appraisal of the contribution that each team member can make, as well as an understanding of their weaknesses and how these can be overcome. For example, a common weakness is in estimating ability. One member of the project team might routinely overestimate how long work will take, whilst another team member underestimates. A project leader who recognizes these problems can identify appropriate situations in which these resources can be applied, and play to their strengths. The over-estimator is given a range of tasks, so the when tasks complete 'early', there is still plenty of work to do, whilst an under-estimator will have contingency assigned to their tasks so that other aspects of the project are not kept waiting when they deliver 'late'.

The leader should review the Project Plan and split tasks so that the most complex tasks can be given to the most skilled team members, whilst leaving plenty of work for the less skilled, who can use these tasks to build their experience and confidence.

Innovating and developing new approaches

In controlling the project, the leader must have confidence and a belief in their own ability so that they are willing to create new ways of working that add to the overall effectiveness of the project team. This requires an open mind and a willingness to consider that what has worked in the past might not be the most appropriate structure for this project. Projects deliver change, and therefore there is no clear picture of what will be created, as it has not existed before. Thus, it cannot be assumed that the management structures that currently exist will necessarily lead to the creative and problem-solving environment that the project requires.

Those responsible for leading programmes must be prepared to establish new organizational structures and assign responsibility and authority levels across the programme organization structure in order for control to be delegated to the most appropriate resources.

The leader must not be unduly concerned with what has gone before, and should recognize that the market conditions and expectations of customers or staff might be so different since the last time a similar project was undertaken that a previous project cannot act as a road map for this one.

The project or programme leader must be prepared to be innovative in their leadership style and the mechanisms that are put in place to coordinate this effort. For example, by developing:

■ New ways of working using different approaches and different techniques
■ New ways of working together – via technology, loosening the boundaries of working hours, working places (from home etc.)
■ New teams and groups to work together
■ Innovative use of advisers and suppliers in the mix of the project board.

Innovation can be hard for the leader to achieve as performing an objective assessment of their management style and identifying changes can fly in the face of the feeling 'if it isn't broken, why fix it?'. However, project leaders must always be aware that not two projects are ever the same, and the conditions for achieving excellence by relying on past successes cannot be guaranteed.

Case study: using a different approach in the new project

Info~U~Want has a policy to ensure that timesheets for temporary resources are authorized by a director before submission to the agency that invoices for the temporary resource. This rule has been established because the employment of temporary resources in the operational environment is regarded as an exceptional measure and is closely monitored as the costs are so much higher than that of a permanent employee. However, taking this approach during the document management project will lead to unnecessary delays for the freelance staff working on the project, especially as the project manager is not a director and therefore has to submit this low-level weekly paperwork to the project sponsor. In this case, the project manager and project sponsor need to agree that the project manager has sign-off authority for all temporary resources working on the project. Although this is going against company policy, it is a sensible response to a common project issue.

3.6 MAKING PROGRESS – PRODUCING THE WORK

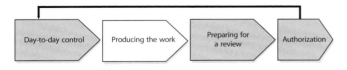

Work in a project is produced by specialist resources, either from within the organization or as members of third-party supplier organizations. Therefore, the leadership challenges at this point in the project centre on the setting of direction and organization of the effort needed for development.

When working with an experienced and knowledgeable project team, the leader must create opportunities for the team members to bond and develop a rapport, which creates trust and team spirit. Once trust has been established, team members will be more willing to contribute to discussions and solve problems in an open manner.

However, at points in the project schedule when there is pressure to deliver against deadlines, the project leader may need to move towards a more decisive and controlling behaviour to ensure there is sufficient focus on delivery.

Those leading in a programme environment will need to create the same type of confident environment between the projects that form the programme as well as within each of the project teams.

Leadership activities required when producing the work in a project

- Ensure that all team members have sufficient autonomy to carry out their work, whilst having sufficient leadership so that they all follow the same direction
- Create an environment where problems can be raised and resolved without blame and recriminations
- Scan the environment for new alliances.

Bringing together the right people

Effective leadership has the confidence to allow the project team members enough autonomy over their roles so that they can develop their own goals. This also encourages the use of their specialist knowledge, which implies that the leader has researched their skills and appreciates what each member of the team can contribute. The leader must actively build connections between the different team members and encourage the development of communities within the team so that the whole is stronger than its parts.

To successfully achieve this, the leader must have a strong sense of their own worth and abilities, but at the same time recognize that their specialist knowledge is not automatically any greater than that of the team members. Therefore, they are able to free themselves from the feeling that productivity would be greater, or quality would be higher, if they did the work themselves. This does not mean that the leader must necessarily be distant from team members. The leader should actively schedule time to coach and mentor team members to increase their skills and their confidence.

This leads to an environment where staff feel empowered to undertake their role, meaning that they are more likely to follow the direction set by the leader rather than fight against it. They can see how they contribute to this direction, and therefore feel a greater ownership over this direction.

Real world experience

'Leadership is about setting the scene, whereas management is about getting the job done. When I am in "leading" mode, it's all about creating the right atmosphere, checking that people are happy with what they are doing, that they feel well informed and involved. When I am in "management" mode, it's about asking for information, analysing situations and deciding on the best course of action.'

Creating the best possible environment to ensure success

In creating this environment, the project leader has two objectives:

■ Providing an environment where all team members feel able to report the truth rather than fabricate results that would look more impressive

■ Providing an environment where team members feel that the information that they provide will be represented honestly and accurately by the project leader.

The trust must go both ways, however, in that the project team must be prepared to trust that any questions that the project leader asks them are not to deliberately find fault, but to enhance understanding across the project. The project leader needs to check that the information they are given is consistent with other information, and continually ask 'Why is that the answer?'.

This trust develops as a result of the responses that the leader gives to team members when information is being presented. Leaders need to show emotional restraint and not allow themselves to display high degrees of bad temper, and indulge in sarcasm, abusive comments or any other examples of emotional bullying. If this is the reaction that a team member receives, it will impact on their willingness to be open and frank with the leader and will inhibit information sharing and the discussion of options. Another important factor in establishing trust is the consistency of the behaviour exhibited by the leader.

Case study: building trust and confidence

If the operations director asks a single member of the project team working on the document management system project to collate all of the intellectual property that exists within Info~U~Want, they may feel daunted by the size of the task, and get off to a slow start as they try different methods for getting the necessary information.

Although the project leader may see the task as relatively simple and straightforward, they must recognize that their feelings are based on past experience of similar projects, which the team member does not have. Instead of stepping in and defining how the work should go, the leader should meet the team member and draw out from them their ideas for approaching the work, help them to break it down into manageable chunks and be willing to review the progress with the team member to provide ongoing encouragement. Whilst this is time-consuming to start with, the project leader will reap the rewards later in the project when they are able to give other, more complex tasks to this team member, who will then have the confidence and the ability to deliver them.

Consistency in leadership

Once work gets under way, the project team and those associated with the project will form an opinion of the leadership style of the project leader. Whatever style is the 'norm', it is helpful if this is maintained, however much pressure the project leader is under. A very strong theme that emerged from all of the interviews for this publication was the need for consistency in leadership style.

Leaders need to recognize that inconsistency between what they say and what they do will be interpreted at best as insincere and at worst duplicitous. There is a need to be open and honest without taking a negative stance. They also need to understand the subliminal messages that are detected when their style changes under pressure.

For example, if part of the leadership style of the project leader involves lots of informal exchanges with project team members and stakeholders, including walking around talking to people, chatting over a cup of coffee, and joining in informal team meetings, then withdrawal of this socialization will send a subliminal message that the leader is under pressure and cannot cope.

Case study: leading under pressure

The operations director is getting a lot of push-back about the project from the other directors and the project team is aware of this. The director should therefore be open about this with the team. Instead of criticizing the other directors in private and denying any knowledge in public, it would be better to acknowledge their opposition and use it as an indicator of areas of the project that need to be improved or better communicated.

The project leader usually has an open-door policy, where any member of the project team or any stakeholder can walk in and discuss their concerns, and they should maintain this even if they feel that the project is hitting crisis point.

To remove the open-door policy will send a message to the followers that the leader cannot cope, or is starting to panic. This is not reassuring, and can evoke a greater need for team members to drop in and share their concerns or seek the support of the project leader. This increases the pressure on the project leader, and can lead to a vicious circle of increasing stress of the leader and the followers.

> **Real world experience**
>
> 'I know this isn't usually a comment about leadership, but I think it's about trust, which is part of leadership. I want my manager to be polite. I want to be thanked for doing a good job, I don't want to be yelled at when things aren't good and I want my hard work acknowledged.'

Creating the best possible environment to ensure success

As a project progresses, difficulties will inevitably arise and the project team will look to their leader to direct them and provide solutions. In many cases, this will possibly require negotiation between different parties.

The leader will have to negotiate a solution, creating value for all parties involved. The first step is to understand the difficulties that each party is facing. The leader must consider the best way to clarify the issue with both parties. Is it wise to bring everyone together straight away, or would it be better to meet each party separately so that they can have a moan and list their concerns without getting heated in front of the other party? Whatever decision is taken, it is important for both parties to have an opportunity to vent their feelings, because until this has happened, they will not be receptive to hearing anything else.

Case study: dealing with setbacks

To test the new document management system at Info~U~Want, real data concerning all of the information held by the different departments will need to be collated and loaded into the system. This is being done at a time when operational staff are working hard to identify new customer opportunities and thus grow the customer base of the organization. This is seen as a priority and any work on the document management system is relegated to a 'best efforts' approach. Without support from the operational staff, the project team is getting behind schedule and tempers are beginning to fray. The project leader brings together the project team and the operational managers to identify a way forward.

In the case of the project team, without the data they cannot test the system, which means that the deadline for the project is being delayed. The operational managers have committed staff to reviewing the customer database for additional opportunities for revenue growth. So, the point of conflict is that the same staff are required for two key initiatives within the organization. The leader will need to emphasize the common ground between the two parties – that they want to deliver the growth plans of the organization – before they can bring the parties together as problem-solving units, working together to solve the same 'growth' problem. Once this basis for negotiation has been established, the leader must ensure that the solution offers value for both parties. In this case, the project teams wish to keep to schedule, and the operational managers wish to identify new customer opportunities. Alternatives for creating this value include:

■ Hiring temporary resources to load the data onto the document management system or to look for new customer opportunities, or to do both

■ Reorganizing the Project Plan so that operational staff have an opportunity to complete some aspects of the customer-related work before dedicating resource to the loading of the document management system.

The operational managers do not wish to cooperate because there is a general feeling of 'we never wanted this system in the first place'. The leader needs to understand that the strategic importance of this project has not been established and its contribution to the growth of the organization has not been accepted. This is a failure from early on in the project lifecycle, and must be addressed otherwise issues of this nature will continue to arise.

Innovating and developing new approaches

The leader has a responsibility to continually scan the environment to develop alliances, and create and operate networks throughout the life of a project, and not just to garner support to get the project off the ground. The project cannot operate in isolation, it must connect with other parts of the organization, and the alliances and the networks that the leader develops is an essential part of this.

> **Real world experience**
>
> 'I think there is some acting involved in being a good leader. In some cases, I have to pretend that I feel calm when I really want to scream. Other times, I have to really look as if I know what I am doing and that I am confident it will work, even though I have never done it before. Leadership is about inspiring confidence in others, and sometimes I have to pretend I have that confidence myself.'

Case study: aligning opinions to project activities

At Info~U~Want, the leader is bringing together people who undertake few if any project activities but are seen as opinion formers within the organization, especially in the areas of:

■ Progress of the project – the ability of the project to contribute to the long-term objectives of the organization. For example, operations managers will volunteer opinions and be asked for information at team meetings by staff who want to know how they are going to be affected by the project. The leader must guide these opinions by:

● Identifying relevant information to share

● Answering any questions promptly

● Identifying linkages, shared interests and common concerns across the opinion formers and helping them develop alliances and user groups to increase staff involvement in the project.

■ Problem-solving – the project leader demonstrates respect for the skills and knowledge of the project team members and gives them as much freedom as possible to solve problems and make decisions. However, these decisions must be taken within the constraints of the project, so there is a reliance on the project leader to ensure that team members are as informed as possible with up-to-date project data.

However, if the team is inexperienced or the project is of critical importance to the organization, the leader may feel the need to adopt a more authoritative stance, dictating the solution to problems and clearly articulating the way forward. For those leading programmes, the challenge is to select an appropriate leadership style for each of the projects within the programme.

3.7 MAKING PROGRESS – PREPARING FOR A REVIEW

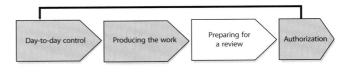

A project is reviewed by the decision-makers at regular points throughout the lifecycle to ensure that:

■ Progress is being made according to plan

■ Products and services developed so far meet the quality criteria set for them

■ Future activities have been appropriately resourced and are still valid

■ The project overall is still viable, i.e. the proposed benefits still outweigh the costs of the project.

Although the project leader should be fully informed of what is happening on the project at any time, preparing for a review provides a useful opportunity to sum up progress so far, and to identify lessons learnt and develop improvements for the future. However, this can cause anxiety for team members, as what they have produced and their approach to their work come under scrutiny.

Leadership activities required when preparing for a review of a project

■ Review progress to assess if the project is still on course to contribute to the realization of the strategic direction of the organization.

Taking a long-range perspective

The project leader must review the progress that the project has made against the strategic objectives of the organization to identify where the project is drifting from this long-range perspective and be prepared to take action to put it back on track. In Figure 3.10, the grey dotted arrows show where a project has deviated from its course to contribute to the strategic objectives of the organization, and the blue dotted arrows indicate when the leader has taken corrective action.

Figure 3.10 Keeping the project or programme aligned to corporate strategy

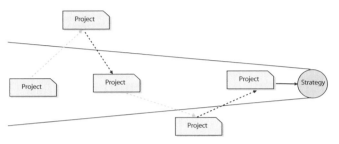

At the same time, the leader must continually be in touch with the strategists and decision-makers within the organization to ensure that the strategy for the organization has not changed (Figure 3.11).

Figure 3.11 Tracking the position of corporate strategy

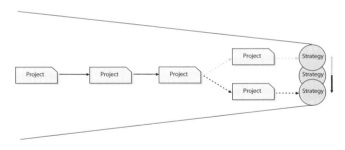

Real world experience

'I try never to apologize for the direction we have taken. "Sorry" is such an emotive word – it makes people think of mistakes or bad behaviour. I would rather thank people for suggesting the new direction and explain why we are taking it rather than apologizing for what has gone before. I think apologies can open us up to blame.'

Scanning the environment thus involves analysing the project information for trends and patterns that may have a wider impact than just the immediate situation within the project. For example, if a project team discovers that the method used by the sales department to classify potential and existing customers is much less detailed than the system used by the operational department, then this will need to be escalated so that an organization-wide decision can be made on the way forward:

- Keep the two methods
- Choose the method from either the sales or the operational department
- Design a completely new approach.

Another example of this 'trend analysis' is risk management. Ensuring that risks are identified, recorded and regularly reviewed is a product of effective project management. However, project leadership means that the source of the risks and the types of risk should be assessed against the strategic direction of the organization, to get a sense of whether or not the operation believes that what is being developed will work in the longer term.

In both of these examples, it is the responsibility of the leader to channel this information into the plans and activities of the project so that the project continues to move in the same long-range direction as the organization.

Gathering information for a project review requires a high degree of cooperation between the project leader and the project team members. The project leader needs to act as a chairperson, gathering information and asking questions that further develop these initial answers. The project team can be encouraged to solve the problems associated with presenting 'bad news' to the decision-makers, and will be motivated by the opportunity to shape the description of 'their' project that is given to the decision-makers.

3.8 MAKING PROGRESS – AUTHORIZATION

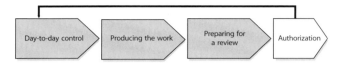

At this point in a project, progress has been made, and the purpose of the authorization is to review whether the project continues to be viable and establish if there is sufficient support across the organization for the project to continue. If the decision-makers do not wish to authorize any further work on the project, it will be prematurely closed and the closing process will be undertaken. Otherwise, the next stage or tranche of work will be authorized by the person responsible for leading the sponsorship of the project and the emphasis moves back to those responsible for the day-to-day leadership of the project.

Leadership activities required when authorizing each stage of a project

■ Create an environment where the decision-makers trust what they are being told

■ Bring together the right people to commit to the project in its next stage.

Creating the best possible environment to ensure success

Whilst the activities of a project have probably been assured during each stage, the project leader must ensure that the decision-makers believe in the information they are being given, and that the integrity of the project leader is established. Integrity and belief will develop over time, but the leader must take care to ensure that information presented to the decision-makers does not contradict itself, or leave questions unanswered.

Real world experience

'I want my sponsor to inspire me and the team. When he just sits there nodding as he listens to how we have overcome problems, I want to shake him. He should be giving us encouragement and helping us appraise how we did so we can learn for the future.'

Sometimes it is worth holding a rehearsal of the authorization meeting with project team members and 'friendly' stakeholders, to ensure that the project leader has all of the information and can answer all of the questions that the decision-makers are likely to pose. This extra effort is often worthwhile for authorization to the next tranche of a programme that requires an explanation of the progress across multiple projects.

The project leader must reassure the decision-makers that there is a balance between external and internal resources so that the culture of the organization is not overrun by high levels of change and issues – for example, ensuring that the transfer of knowledge from the external experts to the internal staff has been planned for. Consideration must be given on how to make external resources integrate into the environment and culture of the organization and become as productive as possible as early as possible.

Case study: using a different approach in the project

At Info~U~Want, it is customary to produce a large project report at each of the interim authorizations. However, the time taken to produce, review, correct and publish this report may be considerable and not the best use of the time available. The leader should address this, perhaps by reassuring the decision-makers that all of the information traditionally put in the report does exist, and show them in which project documents it is held, and create instead a short presentation of key points. Alternatively, the leader might bring along demonstration models of software or other products and give the decision-makers a chance to try things out for themselves.

The main aim at this point in the project lifecycle is to ensure that the decision-makers are still engaged with the project, as once the initial sign-off has been given, momentum and interest can be lost.

Bringing together the right people

Dealing with conflicting and changing opinions

As with all authorizations, this is the point at which the leadership of the day-to-day activities of a project and the leadership of the sponsoring activities intersect. The person responsible for leading the sponsorship of the project must ensure that the project is reviewed by as many of the impacted parties as possible. Those impacted will have formed an opinion as to the value of the project

and this may be different from their earlier views, when the project was only at the ideas stage.

It is possible that the leader will have to debate opinions that were expressed at previous authorizations where stakeholders either tried to include things in the project or programme that were decided to be out of scope or try to remove things from the scope of the project or programme that were included for the benefit of the organization overall.

The leader must have a clear idea of those likely to be for and against continuation of the project before entering this meeting. The leader must establish themselves as the chair of this authorization meeting and, from this position, attempt to control what can be a lively debate.

Figure 3.12 Mapping the direction of support

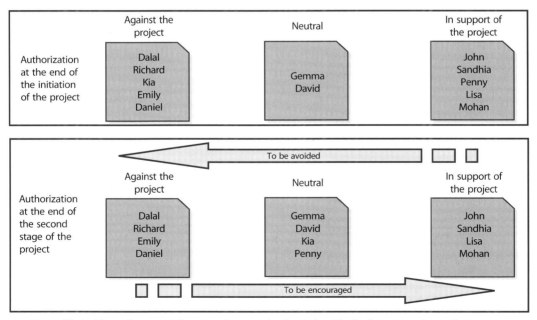

Kia and Penny have moved to neutral support for the project. The leader must understand:
• What factors have motivated these moves
• Who else is likely to be impacted by these factors
• How the factors that led to a move from 'against' to 'neutral' can be enhanced
• How the factors that led to a move from 'in support' to 'neutral' can be minimized.

Building support

In the upper panel of Figure 3.12, the initial positions of those responsible for authorization of a project have been mapped. In the lower panel of the figure, the leader maps the current levels of support. The leader needs to understand the direction of travel in terms of overall levels of support, as well as the individual reasons for these movements, before being able to identify actions to improve the situation. The aim is to move all participants to be in support of the project or programme, or at least be neutral about it.

The leader must fully acquaint themselves with all of the arguments, for and against the project, and understand what is likely to be driving each of these views. It helps to have researched actual examples of why a particular aspect of the project is needed and how it will contribute to the business-as-usual environment. These actual examples should relate to the processes that people understand and should not simply be a financial equation that is hard to engage with on an emotional level.

In a programme environment, developing and maintaining support is a considerable undertaking as there are so many stakeholders whom the leader must influence. In some cases, the stakeholders are not directly impacted by the products or services created by the programme, but are affected by changes to the organizational culture and strategic direction that result from the programme. In these cases, the leader generates support by demonstrating how the programme endorses the values and beliefs of these stakeholders rather than highlighting the benefits of individual tangible deliverables such as new systems or procedures.

Case study: using the 'telling a story' approach to gain support

If the operations director believes that the document management project will save duplication of effort, the director should tell a story that illustrates how frustrating and wasteful duplication really is. In Figure 3.13, each paragraph of the story has a specific purpose. If the initiative was a programme rather than a project, the leader would tell a story about the contribution that the programme is making to the growth of the organization and the expansion of its product range.

Dealing with changing alliances

At authorization meetings, the leader must also demonstrate political awareness. As the reality of the changes that the project is delivering are realized, different alliances may form, especially in operational areas. On a positive note, these alliances may form to exploit the benefits offered by the project, which means these groups may push for enhancement of the scope of the project. On a negative note, alliances may form to 'fight back' against the project as managers begin to understand how their operational duties will be changed once the project has been implemented.

Even if earlier authorizations of the project included significant debate, the leader must recognize that past success is no indicator of future agreement, and therefore they must engage in significant debate to 'win over' and develop as much support from stakeholders as possible. This effort must be a continual process, and cannot occur only at the point that people are drawn together to take decisions about the project. Also, it must continue right up to the point of implementation, otherwise those leading the day-to-day efforts of the project will not have enough support to be successful.

Support for the leader

The leader has a responsibility to lead by example. There is no point in energising stakeholders to give their support to the project if the leader inadvertently undermines the value of the project with ill-timed and ill-considered comments. Leaders feel the pressure of having to lead a project through to success and it is only natural that they will want an outlet to relieve this pressure: a chance to moan about the project team; a chance to criticize and complain about the operational staff not supporting the project; space in which to feel unsure of the probability of success. However, this outlet must be well chosen, to include key factors such that:

- They are trustworthy, so that confidential comments are not relayed to other parties
- They are not impacted by the project in any way
- They are supportive, so that they will listen to the complaints and concerns but be ready to engage in debate to seek solutions and resolve the issues.

The leader needs to select a confidant, or a coach/mentor who can provide this support, and get them ready for the next 'fight' on the project.

Case study: effective leadership takes the project forward

In the document management project, the operations director has fought hard for the support of the other directors in getting this project off the ground. However, the operations director is aware that some managers are still unhappy that their system has not been chosen as the organization-wide solution and other managers are still struggling to see the project as a priority that they should engage with. The operations director has many other responsibilities alongside this project, but when they are in the company of anyone connected with the project, they must remember that they need to feel that the project is their number-one priority.

Figure 3.13 Developing support for a project or programme

Takes action before commissioning the project, showing that the project has been well thought out.

Use of 'I' shows personal involvement which explains his position as sponsor.

Also, the Operations Director uses the word 'problem' so he is giving a strong reason for the project.

'I discovered' relates the story to the Operations Director, giving it a human face that people are able to connect to.

Explaining why Marketing create their report shows that they have a good business reason and that this story is not a criticism of Marketing.

'Before deciding to commission this project, I witnessed first hand some of the problems we have here at Info-U-Want.'

'I asked John in Finance to pull together a report of the staff time and associated costs for all of the research proposals that we wrote for Eastern Europe last year. It took him a couple of weeks, and was a great report.'

'However, the next day, I discovered that this kind of report is routinely put together by Marketing, as they use the information to calculate the cost base for each new campaign that they run.'

'When I told John, he was furious. He felt his time had been wasted and that Finance could really benefit from the reports that Marketing were doing, but had never seen any of them.'

'Marketing were happy to give the information to Finance – they had just never been asked for it before. The new organization-wide document management system will make it easy for all departments to see what work has already been created so that we can all concentrate our efforts on creating new ideas, and not redoing existing work.'

Using the staff member's name makes the story 'personal' so people are able to connect to it.

Saying it was a 'great report' keeps the story positive.

Mentioning John's feelings shows that there is a human cost to this business problem that people can relate to.

Proves that solving the problem does not cause any difficulties, implying there is no reason why the document management project should not be successful.

Leaders must avoid certain types of comments to their own managers:

'I will be so glad when this project is over. It's taking up all my time when there are so many other important things to be doing.'

'I am beginning to doubt that this project is worth all of the effort. I have just had another meeting where all we talked about was the reasons why this project will never be a success.'

If the leader wants commitment for the project, they have to be shown to be committing to it. Examples include: giving up time to attend meetings to support the project team; reading requirements documents or user guides and really engaging with the system that is being created, so that the staff can see that they are taking a tangible interest in the project; helping to find solutions to irritating problems such as not enough meeting rooms to hold a workshop (operations director gives up their own spacious office for the day, and hot desks so that the workshop can go ahead); or making it clear to the senior managers at the supplier companies how important the project is to them, the next time they meet in a social situation.

3.9 CLOSING DOWN – EVALUATION

As a project comes to a close, there is an opportunity to review what has been achieved. Two types of evaluation need to take place for the project:

■ The 'technical' side of project management needs to be evaluated to understand if the project and programme management structure and standards have been followed and to identify if there are any enhancements that would be useful for future projects

■ A content evaluation needs to take place to ensure the 'right' products and services were created, bearing in mind changes to the strategic direction of the organization and the marketplace in which it operates may have altered over the lifetime of the project.

However, evaluation of the leadership of the project should not be overlooked. This is often a personal review of the actions taken by the leader, and involves leaders asking themselves sometimes difficult questions. The ability to conduct a real review of leadership capability involves an open mind, honesty to recognize when things could have gone better and having a sense of self-worth that provides the confidence to carry out the review in the first place.

The person responsible for leading the day-to-day efforts of the project needs to evaluate their leadership of the project team and the operational staff directly impacted by the project. They should examine their success in:

■ Encouraging and motivating the project team to deliver their work and resolve their own issues

■ Developing alliances and networks that contributed support and resources to the project.

The person responsible for leading the sponsorship of the project needs to evaluate their leadership of the project board and the stakeholders connected to the project. This assessment should examine their success in:

■ Engaging and maintaining support for the project

■ Setting a clear and consistent direction for the project

■ Resolving issues and overcoming problems and challenges.

Leadership activities required when evaluating a project

■ Create an environment where people feel able to provide honest feedback about the project

■ Select relevant resources to take part in evaluation.

Creating the best possible environment to ensure success

Evaluation should answer the following questions:

- What could we have done differently?
- What can we do better next time?

The leaders of the sponsorship and the day-to-day effort need to create an environment of continuous learning, where those involved welcome the opportunity to identify the lessons that have been learnt and are willing to participate in identifying improvements for the future.

The atmosphere in which this evaluation is conducted is important because all those involved must feel able to speak freely, without censure. Any criticisms raised by those asked to evaluate the project cannot be taken personally by the project leader, as this will inhibit people from speaking their minds. In some cases, this will require the leader to demonstrate high levels of emotional restraint, and as with other points in the life of the project, the leader may need to 'let off steam' with friends and family in order to maintain this restraint.

The project leader needs to define a structure for the evaluation but the input must come from all those involved and impacted by the project. The project leader will need to utilize all of the networks and alliances built up during the project and will need high levels of 'persuasive' skills to generate contributions. This is particularly true for programmes as the number of people impacted by all of the projects is so high.

People will only want to evaluate the project and give their opinions if they think the information will be used and will make a difference in the future. Therefore, the leader must identify the mechanism by which lessons that have been learnt from this project will be acted on. Therefore, the leader must be willing to direct and encourage this activity, sometimes for a considerable period of time after the project has closed.

Bringing together the right people

Evaluation can be emotional, as those involved find it difficult to see the points being raised as anything other than personal criticism. Therefore, the project leader needs to assess the personality types and behaviour patterns of the project team or project board members, to identify whether the evaluation is best carried out by the teams themselves or via other individuals who were not connected with the project day to day and who did not take decisions relating to the project, and are therefore able to be objective as they are not critiquing their own work.

Evaluating the project can often lack energy and enthusiasm as many of the participants will either have moved onto new projects or are busy learning how to work differently as a result of the project. The leader will need to be creative and develop ways to evaluate the project that are of interest to all those who were involved.

3.10 HANDOVER – LEADING CHANGE

Handover is the point at which the products and services created by a project are released to the operational areas within the organization that will use them. As the project is on the verge of closure, the project leader must turn their attention to inspiring and motivating the adoption of these new products and services.

Case study: handover of the new document management system

The document management project at Info~U~Want is now towards the end of its last stage, and operational staff are being shown the new system, with the objective that they will develop procedures for their departments that will enable them to fully utilize the new system. The project team members are proud of the system that they have developed and are excited that the project is nearly ready to go live. The operational staff feel less enthusiastic as they are conscious of the need to get to know the new system and to change the way they do things.

Leadership activities required when authorizing the closure of a project

- Create an environment where operational staff trust the competency and integrity of the products and services that have been delivered by the project
- Create an environment of innovation, where the products and services created by the project lead to new ideas for service improvements, product development or growth in customers
- Effective handover requires a strong interface with the operational units that will be using the products and services created by the project. The project leader has to explain how these new products and services contribute to the overall strategic goals of the organization.

Creating the best possible environment to ensure success

Operational units are unlikely to make the changes necessary to adopt the outputs from a project unless they feel ownership of them, so it is at this point that the project leader has to move the responsibility for the creation of the future state, and the achievement of the strategic objectives of the organization, from the members of the project team to the staff based in the operational units.

The project leader must work closely with operational managers to build an environment where staff are encouraged to take real ownership of what has been created and adopt it, amend it and apply it as they see fit. It must be clearly demonstrated to staff that they are trusted with this responsibility and that members of the project team are not going to swoop in and take over.

This means that the project leader has to communicate this need to the project team members, and help them to understand that their role is now about knowledge transfer and coaching of operational staff to become fully proficient and self-sufficient in the use of the project outputs.

The project leader has to demonstrate political awareness in identifying those staff within the operational environment who have not only the official authority to take up the adoption of the project outputs, but also have the political support of their colleagues to do so.

Innovating and developing new approaches

Successful handover of new products and services depends on the willingness of operational staff to cast aside their current procedures and develop new approaches and ways of working. The project leader is not responsible for this activity, but can assist by ensuring that messages that come from the project do not emphasize how products are to be used, as innovation will not take place if operational staff feel that the outputs from the project can only be used in specific ways.

The leader must demonstrate an open mind and be tolerant when new ways of working are identified which were never the intention of the project but are still beneficial to the organization. At this point in the project lifecycle, the person responsible for leading the day-to-day effort of the project can no longer rely on the actual authority that their role confers upon them. Instead, they must acquire the necessary authority through the use of persuasion and influencing skills.

Case study: ensuring maximum utilization of the new system

The project manager for the document management system cannot force staff within Info~U~Want to adopt the new system. Each member of staff will decide how much cooperation they are prepared to offer and this will be influenced by the perceived benefits that they associate with the project. To lead staff towards the adoption of the system, the project manager must be prepared to engage in discussion to discover:

- The values and priorities by which staff evaluate the success of their work – for example, the staff in Info~U~Want might judge their success on the quality of the research proposals they create, the timeliness by which they are delivered or their ability to 'go the extra mile' when meeting customer needs.

- The ways in which the project contributes to these values – for example, the system now gives a complete picture of all work planned and completed by the organization. Staff can choose to share this wider appreciation with customers, making the organization appear comprehensive in its product range and making the staff member look well informed.

- The impediments that prevent the document management system from improving service – for example, because of the amount of data in the system, the response times are slower than intended, but this can be improved through a simple change to the way reports are produced.

3.11 CLOSING DOWN – AUTHORIZATION

At this point in a project lifecycle, authorization is sought to close the project and officially disband the project team.

Leadership activities required when authorizing the closure of a project

- Take a long-range perspective of how the new products and services delivered by the project contribute to the ability of the organization to realize its strategic objectives.

Taking a long-range perspective

At this point, the two forms of project leadership that have been operating during the project lifecycle come together to ensure there are no loose ends and that the long-range perspective that was identified and articulated at the start of the project has been delivered.

The person responsible for leading the sponsorship of the project can choose to use the announcement of the closure to clarify to the organization as a whole how the project actually helps the organization deliver its strategic objectives. This is dependent on the quality of the information that they receive, which is in part controlled by the person who has led the day-to-day efforts on the project. This leader has a responsibility to assess the contribution that the project has made, and not simply report on what has been undertaken. Too often, those involved in the project will articulate the effort that has been made in terms of time taken, money spent, resources used and outputs created, at the expense of asking 'What has changed as a result of this project?'.

Appendices

Appendix A: Prioritizing leadership activities

Appendix A provides advice on how to prioritize leadership activities and maintain a leadership approach whilst under the pressure of being a project leader.

Project leadership activities are underpinned by an ongoing evaluation of the project to ensure it is heading in the right direction, has the necessary support and that the direction is understood by all those working on or impacted by the project. There is also the need to assess how the 'followers' are feeling, and assess their level of support. There are a number of challenges associated with prioritizing leadership activities above other types of project or programme activity:

- Maintaining the effort of leadership throughout the project lifecycle
- Finding sufficient time to be a leader
- Listening more than talking.

A.1 MAINTAINING THE EFFORT OF LEADERSHIP THROUGHOUT THE PROJECT LIFECYCLE

Leadership involves shaping the views and opinions of staff and other stakeholders over a concerted period of time, as buy-in, motivation and support can rarely be achieved at one sitting.

The ongoing nature of many of the leadership activities presents its own challenges, particularly for project leaders who are under pressure to deliver the project within an agreed timeframe and therefore do not have the luxury of playing the waiting game. If a people-related issue has not been solved and is still simmering within the project, a great deal of skill and self-discipline must be shown by the project leader to put that issue on hold, move on

and deal with other situations, and judge when it would be most appropriate to pick up and run with the original issue again.

A.2 FINDING SUFFICIENT TIME TO BE A LEADER

Practically, this means that the leader must build in sufficient time to assess the situation, analyse the data, think through any issues and take the necessary action. Leadership is not all about 'doing the work', and therefore the time required to understand the context, think, plan and strategize should be prioritized as highly as more obvious project activities.

One of the challenges, however, is that too often in a project or programme environment, those in a leadership role are judged on their levels of activity, and the visible progress that they make (giving presentations, chairing meetings, creating plans and reports), rather than on the quality of their low-key leadership interventions.

In order to set aside sufficient time, the project leader must be honest with themselves about how they work, and understand and appreciate how they like to tackle the different leadership activities. For example, a leader should know their preferred working style, from whether they are a morning person, to whether they prefer to work in an open-plan space or a small private office. They must understand their preferred style of interaction with people – face-to-face meetings or a more distant issuing of written instructions and commentary.

Whilst leadership is about embodying certain characteristics and displaying certain personality traits and is therefore constant and ongoing, it is still important to put time in the diary to be a leader. Leaders must understand the type of activities that they are likely to perform, and estimate where possible the time involved in these activities. One way to achieve this is to create a leadership strategy that sets out how these activities will be carried out and what outputs or resources are expected from each activity.

As shown in the example in Table A.1, the activities would need to be scheduled into any week during the life of the project, including time for any follow-up actions that result from undertaking these activities.

The weekly hours required to follow this leadership strategy reveals that approximately half of the working week would be spent on these planned leadership activities. This underlines the difference between leadership and management and gives an indication of how much self-discipline needs to be given to maintaining a leadership approach.

Table A.1 An example leadership strategy

Activity	Time required	Scheduling needs
Leading and developing the project team		
Holding group 'teach ins' to develop specific project skills including risk management, planning, budgeting	One hour per week on a group basis	Can be combined with normal team meetings
Reviewing the roles of each of the team members and developing goals that not only stretch them but also add to the overall ability of the team	30 minutes per month on an individual basis	One-to-one with the individuals concerned
Identifying examples of team communication and problem-solving that are to be praised and held up as examples of how things should be done	30 minutes a week to identify good examples	Can be combined with normal team meetings
Identify areas where the team has failed to perform satisfactorily and work with the team to clarify what should be done in similar circumstances in the future	30 minutes a week to identify areas for improvement	One-to-one with the individuals concerned
One-to-one coaching and/or mentoring of project team members as part of their ongoing development	One hour per fortnight on an individual basis	One-to-one with the individuals concerned

Table A.1 continued

Activity	Time required	Scheduling needs
Identifying areas of concern		
Providing direction for assigning time and priority to different project tasks	Two hours per week	Coaching to be spread across the project team members
Identifying if the project is ahead of, on or behind schedule and understanding the factors that have led to this situation	Four hours per week	Quiet reflection and also takes place at team meetings
Identifying factors/issues that will arise in the near future that could impact on the progress of the project	Three hours per week	This is an essential leadership activity that cannot be skipped even in busy weeks
Putting in place communications that will ensure that relevant team members are aware of these circumstances and take actions to overcome them (via team meetings, risk management workshops etc.)	One hour per meeting multiplied by the number of meetings	Meetings for each topic
Developing connections and alliances		
Identifying the corporate networks that the project stakeholders are tapped into	One hour per week for identification	This analysis helps the leader identify at what events the project must be represented
Assessing these networks for opportunities and liaising with members for opportunities to attend and present to them	One hour per week for assessment – up to six hours a week in attendance	This should be a significant portion of any week
Finding any forums or associations run by experts in the purpose of the project and attending events to develop a network of experts upon whom the project can call if needed	Three hours per week	This may involve evening events

A.3 LISTENING MORE THAN TALKING

An effective leader will recognize that information from all stakeholders is essential in leading the project successfully. A leader has to create opportunities for listening – formally as well as informally. Formal opportunities occur at meetings, workshops and presentations, but the informal opportunities to listen to what people think – when they are at the coffee machine, getting into the lift or leaving the building at the end of the day – are also important.

Appendix B: Chairing meetings, taking decisions, and using influencing and negotiating skills

This appendix gives guidance on how to undertake the key leadership activities of chairing meetings and taking decisions, and the benefits and use of influencing and negotiating skills.

B.1 CHAIRING A DISCUSSION

There are many points during the project lifecycle when the leader will need to chair a debate or a discussion. This is especially true as project leadership often requires a democratic leadership style, where participants take part in a forum to express their views, hear the views of others and make a conscious decision to sign up to the project objectives and understand their contribution to these objectives.

Before chairing any kind of discussion, it is essential to be clear about the purpose of the event. In some cases, it is sensible to bring people together to share their thoughts and ideas, and enhance the understanding of all those involved. In other cases, whilst it is still important to share knowledge, the purpose of the event is to come to a decision about the direction of the project or the next steps to be taken.

In order for the event to be successful, there are some basic rules to follow. Some of these are common sense, and some of these have been identified by the interviewees for this publication as essential for keeping things on track and preventing emotion from dominating the proceedings.

Establish the chair of the discussion prior to the event

The chair does not necessarily have to be the acknowledged leader of the project. In a discussion which is primarily about information sharing, someone who has a great deal of technical or specialist knowledge might be a sensible choice, as they can steer the conversations in a logical and sensible direction, relevant to the topic being discussed.

However, when the primary objective of the event is to take a decision on the direction of the project, then the discussion must be chaired by the project leader.

A suggested role description for the chairperson is:

- Leading and managing the business of the meeting to provide clear direction and focus
- Ensuring that meetings are properly chaired, structured and run in accordance with agreed parameters
- Setting the agenda, style and tone of project discussions to promote fast and effective decision-making
- Facilitating constructive discussion amongst project team members and other stakeholders
- Ensuring that the strategies and actions approved by the meeting are effectively implemented by the relevant project team members
- Working closely with the project team members to provide support and advice whilst respecting their responsibilities for day-to-day management of the project activities

■ Addressing the development needs of the project team with a view to enhancing its overall team effectiveness.

Identify an agenda and circulate it prior to the event

If the discussion is about knowledge sharing, it is still important to give some structure to the event, otherwise it will be very difficult to involve everyone and to bring the discussion to a close.

Identify key areas of the project that would benefit from clarification, and set these out in a logical sequence – for example, based on when they occur in the project lifecycle. Set some guidance for how long each point is to be discussed, and be clear about the start and end times of the discussion. This will enable the participants to book suitable time to attend, and it minimizes the number of attendees who discover they have to leave early or cannot attend the first part. These disruptions make the role of chair very difficult, as there is a need to conclude the current discussion before the participant leaves prematurely, and also requires a summary of where the discussion has reached before 'new joiners' can be fully integrated into the event.

Use the invitation to develop an atmosphere of inclusion

Generally speaking, everyone likes to feel wanted and involved in an undertaking so it is worth using the invitation to a discussion or debate to ensure that those impacted by the project feel involved and valued. If the purpose of the discussion is to share information, then this is relatively easy. However, if the purpose is to come to a conclusion, it is important to establish criteria to limit those invited to attendees who have the authority to make decisions. There may be others who would like to be involved, but they do not actually have the power of decision making in connection with the project and so do not have a role to play. As this can be a divisive statement, the leader may have to hold a 'softer' discussion event to which a wide audience is invited, before holding a second, more 'closed' event that only the decision-makers attend.

Be hospitable

Pick a room that is suitable for the size and format of the event. If the discussion is to be led by a presentation of some kind, ensure there is space and equipment if necessary. Simple issues of hospitality (or the lack of) can set the tone of the event. Experience shows that the more respect we show our colleagues, the more respectfully they will behave, however heated the subject. Therefore, the more sensitive the issues being debated, the more important it is to ensure everyone has sufficient room, there are refreshments and access to pens and paper etc.

Arrive early

If you are the chair of the discussion, get to the event early and make sure you greet each person as they arrive. It is possible that participants may wish to make you aware of new information, or a particular point of contention prior to speaking more publicly and this is a good opportunity to allow this to occur.

Call on everyone

Ensure each person has a chance to voice their opinion. A number of people taking part in the discussion will not need any encouragement, but it is helpful to solicit the views of those who are staying quiet as well. A simple question such as 'John, you have been listening very attentively so far, is there anything you would like to add?' can be very effective.

Record the event

For a knowledge-sharing event, consider how a record of the knowledge can be provided to those who have taken part, and disseminated to a wider audience if appropriate.

For example, if flipcharts or whiteboards have been used to take notes in the discussion, can these be typed up after the event and sent out. If the event is decision-based, consider asking a member of the project team to take the minutes in a way that records the elements of the discussion and the strength of support for the decision.

Limit opinions and encourage facts

This basic rule applies to knowledge-sharing events as well as decision-based events. Whatever the subject, encourage the speaker to support the point they are making with an example, or present the results of a study or numbers from the corporate reporting system. This ensures a more objective view is expressed, and discourages the development of entrenched opinions which speakers then find it difficult to move away from.

Intervene when discussion moves to argument

Argument is an important part of debate. However, time is wasted and relationships can be put under strain when a debate becomes too heated. This is often the result of entrenched opinions on either side.

As the leader, it is important to acknowledge the value in both opinions (if that is the case) or find a sensitive way of closing down the opinion that runs counter to the direction of the project. The leader must step into the discussion at this point, and the easiest way to achieve this is to state your aim of 'summarizing the position so far', as this is always welcomed by the other participants who might either be mystified as to why things are so heated, or have switched off as the argument does not involve them.

As the leader, it is important to bring the discussion back to the original agenda item, and to reignite the involvement of all those attending. To start with, both opinions must be acknowledged and the speakers must be thanked for their contribution. Move on swiftly to the next point, before the argument starts up again; but if that happens, either restate the position and evidence that you have just given, or offer to take the discussion off-line after the event.

In a heated debate, it is not always possible to pinpoint when an argument has become circular, or that the same points are being repeated without conclusion. However, once this point has been identified, consider closing the discussion and scheduling another meeting, or creating a physical break (coffee break, for example) and reframing the point of the discussion once everyone reassembles.

Clarify the conclusion

Establish that the agenda has been completed. Sum up the key points, and acknowledge any outstanding points and what action will be taken about those points, by whom and by when. Thank people for taking part and clarify what happens next, even if all that will happen is that they will be sent the minutes or a record of the knowledge that has been shared.

Do:

■ Respect the contribution of other speakers

■ Speak pleasantly and with courtesy to all members of the group

■ Listen well to the ideas of other speakers; you will learn something

■ Remember that a discussion is not a fight. Learn to disagree politely

■ Respect that others have differing views and are not necessarily 'wrong'

■ Think about your contribution before you speak. How best can you answer the question or contribute to the topic?

■ Stick to the discussion topic. Don't introduce irrelevant information

- Be aware of your body language when you are speaking. Keep it open and friendly, and avoid gestures that appear aggressive
- Agree with and acknowledge what you find interesting
- Stay with the topic. If the discussion does digress, bring it back on topic by saying something like 'Just a final point about the last topic before we move on' or 'That's an interesting point, can we come back to that later?'
- Speak clearly. Don't whisper – even if you're feeling uncertain about your ideas or language.

Don't:

- Take offence if a person disagrees with you. There will be times when other speakers will have different points of view. They may disagree with your ideas, and they are entitled to do so
- Ridicule the contribution of others. Don't use comments like 'That's stupid', That's ridiculous, or 'You're wrong'
- Intimidate or insult another speaker
- Use a loud or angry tone. Others will not want to listen to you if you are being aggressive. Use a moderate tone and medium pitch
- Use negative body language when speaking. Gestures such as finger-pointing and table-thumping appear aggressive
- Dominate the discussion. Confident speakers should allow quieter staff a chance to contribute
- Draw too much on personal experience or anecdote
- Interrupt or talk over another speaker. Let them finish their point before you start. Listening to others earns you the right to be heard.

B.2   DECISION-MAKING

Decisions are a position or opinion or judgement reached after consideration, and they are an integral part of leadership. Many of the decisions that a project leader faces will be new, in as much as the products and services that the project is producing are new to the organization. In order to demonstrate effective leadership, a project leader must have a robust process in place for monitoring and analysing information and selecting from a range of possible options.

Clarify the decision

The leader must understand what needs to be decided at this particular point in the lifecycle of the project:

- Scheduling decision – what activity must come first?
- Resourcing decision – who is best placed to do the work?
- Problem-solving decision – what is the best option to solve the problem?

It is important to break down the decision into several individual decisions. For example, deciding how to get a piece of work finished by the end of the week might involve taking scheduling and resourcing decisions and a problem-solving decision related to the delay from one of the suppliers.

Clarify any assumptions

Failed decision-making is often the result of incorrect assumptions. For example, a decision to hire an expert project planner to develop and maintain all Project Plans has been based on the assumption that no-one with these skills exists within the organization. However, a quick chat with the human resources department would have revealed that three staff had recently attended an intensive planning course.

Develop options

In order to select from a range of possible options, it is important to ensure that the widest range of options have been identified in the first place. In terms of leading projects, there are usually four areas from which these options can be drawn:

- Change the timeframe
- Change the budget
- Change the scope of what the project will deliver
- Change the level of quality that the scope will be delivered to.

There is always a fifth option – to not do the project or to close the project with immediate effect – but we will assume for the purpose of this exercise that the objective is to resolve whatever the situation is, without resorting to non-delivery of the project.

Options are identified based on past experience, and seeing what has worked before in different situations. Therefore, it makes sense to ask for ideas from as many people as possible, to ensure the inclusion of as many different experiences. However, the project leader will need to balance this desire for inclusion against the political concerns that may be raised by senior management, or making problems public and involving stakeholders who might be better served by being presented with solutions rather than becoming involved in problem-solving.

Evaluate the options

Once a range of ideas has been gathered, they need to be assessed for their ability to solve the problem. There are benefits to standardizing this process where possible, as it is easier to see the value of an option, and the problems associated with it, if each option is judged on a like-for-like basis. There are also benefits in terms of organizational learning, as a structured approach will identify factors that can be applied to future projects, and improve the decision-making across the project and programme environment, and not just provide assistance to one particular project.

To assess each option, consider the advantages and disadvantages that its implementation would bring to the project (Table B.1). Give each advantage and disadvantage a value, so that they can be compared. For example, if the project is falling behind schedule, several options can be identified to bring the project back on track, such as:

- Reducing the scope of the project, and concentrating project team efforts on a smaller amount of work
- Increasing the budget of the project so that there is sufficient funding to bring on additional temporary resources to take part in the project activities.

Look for as many implications of this option as possible and decide if the implication is positive or negative in terms of the direction of the organization (not just the health of the project). Give each of these a weighting – to keep it simple use a scale ranging from 1 (weak advantage or disadvantage) to 3 (strong advantage or disadvantage).

In the example in Table B.1, the advantages of de-scoping the project outweigh the advantages of hiring temporary resources, whilst the disadvantages for hiring temporary resources outweigh the disadvantages of de-scoping the project. Therefore, the decision is to de-scope the project.

If at the end of the exercise, the option selected does not fit with the 'gut feeling' of the project leader, then another review should take place, and the project leader should ask if the analysis includes all of the emotional or political implications, i.e. the people-oriented implications, which are often difficult to express or give a value to. Add these in and review the totals for a second time.

Finally, if the option indicated by this process still does not fit with the underlying views of the project leader, he or she should consider talking the situation through with a colleague who is not directly connected with the project to see if they can provide any reasons why the project leader is having a strong reaction against the apparently favourable option.

Table B.1 Scoring advantages and disadvantages of different options

Getting temporary resources		De-scoping the project	
Advantages	**Value**	**Advantages**	**Value**
Enables original deadline to be met	3	Enables original deadline to be met	3
Supports business as usual activities by reducing the need to second operational staff onto the project	2	Does not impact the budget of the project	3
TOTAL	**5**	**TOTAL**	**6**

Disadvantages	**Value**	**Disadvantages**	**Value**
Untrained temporary resources will require additional management time which would be more productively spent leading the project	2	Does not deliver all products and services expected by the users	3
Additional budget for this project means that budgets for other project work will have to be cut	3	Interdependencies between this project and other projects within the organization may be affected	1
Creates a company precedent that additional funding will be given to projects that are struggling to meet their deadlines	1		
TOTAL	**6**	**TOTAL**	**4**

Decision-making using this structure is not foolproof but it does provide an audit trail of how you got to the solution. There is also benefit in applying this same structure to all project-related decisions, as there is commonality about how each conclusion was reached, and it is easy to see at a later stage why a decision turned out to be the wrong one, because the implications can be reviewed and the 'missing data' can be spotted with the power of hindsight.

B.3   INFLUENCING SKILLS

'The act or power of producing an effect without apparent exertion of force or direct exercise of command.' *(Merriam-Webster Dictionary)*

Good leaders characteristically have good influencing skills, which they use to persuade others to move towards their way of thinking, to increase their support base or reduce opposition. This requires having a flexible attitude in terms of choosing the best style of presenting ideas to the situation and the person you want to influence, the resilience to 'think on your feet' and take a fresh approach to tackling difficult situations.

Although influencing and negotiating skills are often linked together, there is a slight and important difference. Whilst influencing centres around the effect words and behaviours can have on another person's beliefs, negotiation involves reaching a common understanding between two parties. This usually means there is some compromise or exchange of values between the two sides. When using influencing skills, one only hopes to persuade another's beliefs or attitudes. However, when using negotiation, both parties should expect to give up something to achieve a mutually beneficial agreement.

The sponsor and decision-makers may need to be influenced to authorize the project, release more resources or take decisions more quickly. The team managers may need to be influenced to work faster, work harder or cooperate better with other teams. And just as importantly, stakeholders outside the team may need to be influenced to get involved, commit to or show support for the project idea.

When attempting to influence another person it is important to understand where that person currently stands on the spectrum of agreement (Figure B.1). The spectrum ranges from being in total agreement to being diametrically opposed to your point of view. If the other person is in total disagreement, then it is unlikely that they can be moved to a position of total agreement. The best that can be hoped for by influencing them is to move them towards your direction and to open them up to the possibilities of thinking differently. A strong influencer can realistically expect to persuade the other person one or two positions to the right, to be more in agreement or at least to take a neutral stance than would have been the case without the influencing activities.

Influencing requires research into the understanding of the other person's viewpoints. Understanding their beliefs and attitudes will help in deciding on the best approach to take. The approach to influencing should include how to communicate and how to behave. If the approach is incorrect, then the person might be negatively influenced, meaning they might move in the direction opposite to that intended.

Once the starting point has been established, the influencer needs to determine how best to convey their message. By opening with common ground that both parties share, the idea of shared interests can be introduced and relationship building between the parties started. Demonstrating empathy and showing appreciation also helps make a human connection. Using language that the other person understands and is familiar with helps bridge differences. Criticism and alienation of the other party should be avoided at all costs. For example, both project and programme managers experience the pressures of delivering their work to budget and time constraints. If a programme manager wishes to influence the way in which a project manager is approaching their work, a good way of first establishing common ground would be to exchange information about how difficult they are finding it to manage their workloads.

The best one can hope for with the use of influencing skills is to move the other person closer to your way of thinking. It is unlikely that the other person will completely abandon their own beliefs and values, but small changes are better than nothing. If small changes are not sufficient for the progress of the project, the influencer may need to change tactics and open up a more formal negotiation process to obtain bigger changes.

Figure B.1 The spectrum of agreement

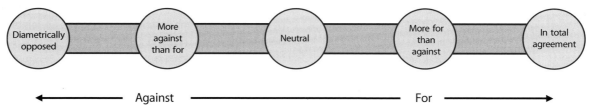

B.4 NEGOTIATING SKILLS

Negotiation happens on an informal basis throughout the project lifecycle but the project leader may also decide to formally apply the principles of negotiation at any point when their ability to influence the other party is not achieving the desired result. The key difference between influencing and negotiating is that influencing relies on persuasion and changing the perceptions of the other party, whereas negotiating requires an exchange of values between the two parties. Applying the latter, both parties are able to feel they achieved their desired results but at the same time did not give away what was of critical value to them, whether it was a principle or some material measure.

Negotiation consists of a four-step process of planning, connection, proposals and agreement. In any one negotiation situation, these steps are repeatable and to be successful may require several attempts at one or more of the steps before both parties can reach a satisfactory resolution. It is important to remember that both parties share a common goal – of reaching an agreement – so that going through the sometimes laborious process will be worth it for both sides.

Step 1 – planning

The first step is to perform sufficient planning of an organized and practical approach to the negotiation. The majority of effort should be spent performing this step. By doing the groundwork first, the subsequent discussions with the other party can run smoothly. Similar to influencing, the planning step requires some preliminary investigation and research to understand the starting position of the other side. By exploring their background you can understand what issues are the most important to them and where there might be some leeway. For example, if a project sponsor is adamant and uncompromising about meeting a specific deadline, they may be willing to concede on the costs to achieve it. However, without this prior knowledge and

understanding, the negotiator will be at a disadvantage when encountering the project sponsor, as they will have to speculate on which aspects are important and which are not. If they misread the situation or are misled, it can be detrimental to the success of the outcome.

A checklist (see box) for preparing for a negotiation helps to ensure that all relevant aspects have been considered prior to the negotiation meeting.

Step 2 – connection

Once the planning has been completed, the next step is to open a channel of communication so the two parties can begin to make a connection. The parties should meet face to face to establish this connection. Communicating electronically or in written form may invite too many opportunities for miscommunication, which can be detrimental to the negotiation process. If the parties are not able to build a rapport by focusing on their similar interests and common goals, then the process may end here and require escalation to senior management. By making this connection, both sides can judge first-hand how willing the other side is to finding a resolution to their situation. It may be quite telling at this early stage when one or both sides deliberately misleads or withholds information as to how the rest of the process will continue.

Step 3 – proposals

After the connection has been made, the next step in the negotiation is to open up the discussion to allow for initial proposals of solutions. This may take several iterations of proposals, consideration, compromise and concession before an agreeable outcome can be reached. Negotiation issues for a project or programme tend to centre on time, cost, quality and scope. Different stakeholders have varying opinions about what should be included or excluded from the initiative, which may result in a roadblock for all or part of the effort. The best possible outcome of a negotiation is a 'win-win' solution, where both parties feel that their needs were met without harming their relationship.

Negotiation preparation checklist

1 Understand your own needs:

■ What is the ideal result you are looking for from this negotiation?

■ Where is there room to compromise from this ideal?

■ Research different options that may be just as suitable.

2 Understand the needs of the other side:

■ Investigate their current situation – financial, political, logistical, legal etc.

■ Study the outcomes of previous negotiations held by the other side

■ Speculate what the ideal outcome the other side requires

■ Determine what they might be willing to concede

■ Brainstorm different options from their perspective.

3 Estimate the most likely intersection of both parties' needs:

■ Prioritize the needs of both sides

■ Based on your research of the other side and your understanding of your own needs, estimate a likely compromise for each need

■ What are the must-haves and what are the nice-to-haves?

■ Which of the four project elements is the most important – time, cost, quality or scope?

■ How far can each of these elements be stretched before the viability of the project ceases to exist?

■ What is the value that cannot be compromised on as a result of this negotiation?

4 Practise for the event:

■ Rehearse the negotiation meeting at least once, although preferably several times with different outcomes

■ Be prepared to deal with new information as it arises

■ Before moving on to the next step, clearly understand what is more important to you – the current relationship with the other side or the outcome?

Step 4 – agreement

When conducting a formal negotiation with third-party suppliers or partnership transactions, it is regarded as best practice to document the agreement in writing. Having written evidence of the agreement, such as a contract, which both parties are required to sign, can eliminate problems further down the line. When conducting an informal negotiation with team managers or other projects within the organization, a written contract may not be required; instead a verbal agreement may be sufficient, usually followed by an email providing the details that were agreed. If a satisfactory agreement cannot be reached, then the process may need to start again or at least return to a previous step. Escalation to senior management may be required if the process delays the project timeline or the parties are stymied at an impasse.

Appendix C: Comparison of leadership styles against the culture of the organization and the importance of the project

In this appendix, the characteristics of three very common leadership styles have been illustrated against the culture of the organization in which the leader is operating and the importance and urgency of the project to be delivered. Leaders do not apply one leadership style to all situations and Table C.1 illustrates the different features of these styles and how they might apply as the project progresses. For example, the leader may start off with a laissez-faire approach but this will move over time to a more autocratic style as the project begins to run late and the leader has less time for consultation. However, the leader can only go so far towards an autocratic style, because they need to take into account the culture of the organization, which might not support this style.

Table C.1 Leadership styles

	Autocratic	**Democratic**	**Laissez-faire**
Culture of the organization	Managers have tight control over the work and actions of the staff	Control over resources is decided via negotiation and influencing, rather than being imposed in an hierarchical structure	There is light control over the work and the actions of staff and a high degree of trust between colleagues
	There is a strong hierarchical structure and the amount of authority that each manager has is governed by their seniority within the organization	Authority is the result of knowing whom to influence and the creation of different power bases within the organization	Authority is derived from skills and experience and not the job title or length of service within the organization
Importance and urgency of the project	The project is driven by a legal requirement that must be satisfied by a specific date, or seeks to exploit an opportunity that will only be available for a set period of time	The project is driven by the need to create efficiencies or cost savings within the organization that will enable funding to become available for other initiatives	The project is driven by an idea and is speculative
	Funding for the project takes advantage of a pool of money that is only available within a specified period of time	The area of business impacted by the business will still continue to exist, even if the project cannot demonstrate the anticipated cost/time savings	The results will deliver a proof of concept that can be developed into a full blown project at a later date

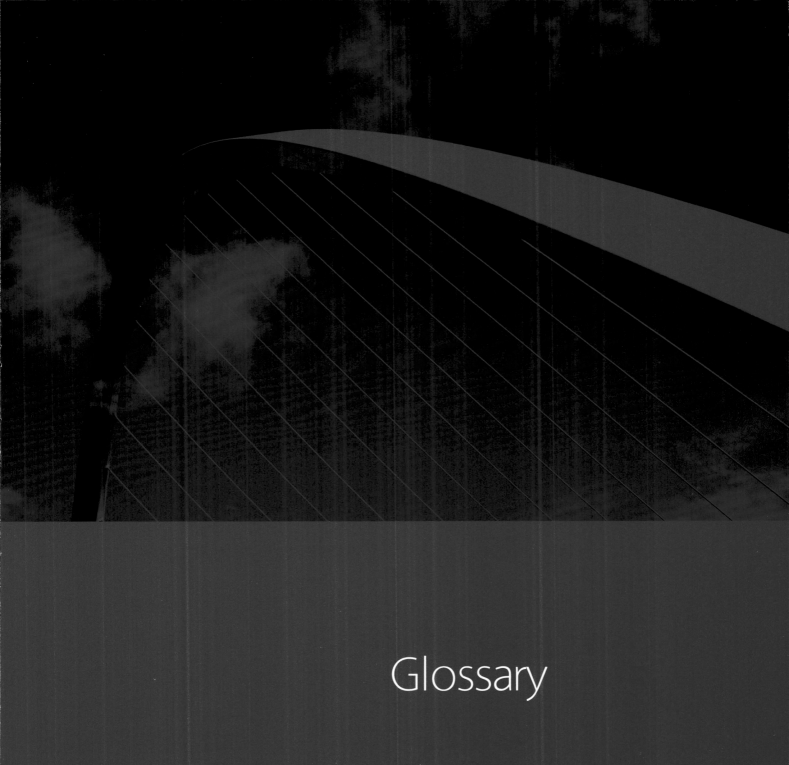

Glossary

Glossary

Activity
An activity is a process, function or task that occurs over time, has recognizable results and is managed.

Benefit
The measurable improvement resulting from an outcome perceived as an advantage by one or more stakeholders.

Business as usual
The way the business normally achieves its objectives.

Business Case
The justification for an organizational activity (strategic, programme, project, operational) which typically contains costs, benefits, risks and timescales and against which continuing viability is tested.

Business change manager
The role responsible for benefits management, from identification through to realization, ensuring the implementation and embedding of the new capabilities delivered by the projects. Typically allocated to more than one individual. Alternative title: 'change agent'.

Capability
A service, function or operation that enables the organization to exploit opportunities.

Customer
The person or group who commissioned the work and will benefit from the end results.

Deliverable
An item that the project has to create as part of the requirements. It may be part of the final outcome or an intermediate element on which one or more subsequent deliverables are dependent. According to the type of project, another name for a deliverable is 'product'.

Executive
The single individual with overall responsibility for ensuring that a project meets its objectives and delivers the projected benefits. This individual should ensure that the project or programme maintains its business focus, that it has clear authority and that the work, including risks, is actively managed. The executive is the chairperson of the Project Board, representing the customer and owner of the Business Case.

Impact
Impact is the result of a particular threat or opportunity actually occurring.

Issue
A relevant event that has happened, was not planned, and requires management action. Could be a problem, query, concern, change request or risk that has occurred.

Opportunity
An uncertain event that could have a favourable impact on objectives or benefits.

Outcome
The result of change, normally affecting real-world behaviour and/or circumstances. Outcomes are desired when a change is conceived. Outcomes are achieved as a result of the activities undertaken to effect the change. In a programme, the outcome is the manifestation of part or all of the new state conceived in the blueprint.

Output
The tangible or intangible product resulting from a planned activity.

Plan
A detailed proposal for doing or achieving something detailing the what, when, how and by whom.

Policy

A course of action (or principle) adopted by an organization. A business statement of intent, setting the tone for an organization's culture.

Process

That which must be done to bring about a particular result in terms of information to be gathered, decisions to be made and results to be achieved.

Product

An input or output, whether tangible or intangible, that can be described in advance, created and tested. Also known as an output or deliverable.

Programme

A temporary flexible organization structure created to coordinate, direct and oversee the implementation of a set of related projects and activities in order to deliver outcomes and benefits related to the organization's strategic objectives. A programme is likely to have a life that spans several years.

Programme management

The coordinated organization, direction and implementation of a dossier of projects and activities that together achieve outcomes and realize benefits that are of strategic importance.

Programme manager

The role responsible for the set-up, management and delivery of the programme, typically allocated to a single individual.

Programme organization

How the programme will be managed throughout its lifecycle, the roles and responsibilities of individuals involved in the programme, and personnel management or human resources arrangements.

Project

A temporary organization that is created for the purpose of delivering one or more business products according to a specified Business Case.

Project issue

A term used to cover any concern, query, Request for Change, suggestion or off-specification raised during a project. They can be about anything to do with the project.

Project lifecycle

The period from the start up of a project to the handover of the finished product to those who will operate and maintain it.

Project management

The planning, monitoring and control of all aspects of the project and the motivation of all those involved in it to achieve the project objectives on time and to the specified cost, quality and performance.

Project manager

The person given the authority and responsibility to manage the project on a day-to-day basis to deliver the required products within the constraints agreed with the Project Board.

Project Plan

A high-level plan showing the major products of the project, when they will be delivered and at what cost. An initial project plan is presented as part of the Project Initiation Document. This is revised as information on actual progress appears. It is a major control document for the Project Board to measure actual progress against expectations.

Risk

An uncertain event or set of events which, should it occur, will have an effect on the achievement of objectives. A risk is measured by a combination of the probability of a perceived threat or opportunity occurring and the magnitude of its impact on objectives.

Risk management

The systematic application of principles, approach and processes to the tasks of identifying and assessing risks, and then planning and implementing risk responses.

Senior responsible owner

The single individual with overall responsibility for ensuring that a project or programme meets its objectives and delivers the projected benefits.

Sponsor

The main driving force behind a programme or project.

Sponsoring group

The main driving force behind a programme who provide the investment decision and top-level endorsement of the rationale and objectives of the programme.

Stage

A stage is the section of the project that the project manager is managing on behalf of the Project Board at any one time, at the end of which the Project Board may review progress to date, the state of the Project Plan, Business Case and risks, and the next stage plan in order to decide whether to continue with the project.

Stakeholder

Any individual, group or organization that can affect, be affected by, or perceive itself to be affected by, an initiative (programme, project, activity, risk).

Strategy

The approach or line to take, designed to achieve a long-term aim. Strategies can exist at different levels in an organization – in Managing Successful Programmes there are corporate strategies for achieving objectives that will give rise to programmes. Programmes then develop strategies aligned with these corporate objectives against particular delivery areas.

Supplier

The group or groups responsible for the supply of the project's specialist products.

Tranche

A group of projects structured around distinct step changes in capability and benefit delivery.

Index

Index